HANDBOOK FOR SPIRITUAL DIRECTORS

BY

JULIE M. DOUGLAS

PAULIST PRESS
New York/Mahwah, NJ

Library of Congress Cataloging-in-Publication Data

Douglas, Julie M.,   1949–
   Handbook for spiritual directors / by Julie M. Douglas.
     p.   cm.
   Includes bibliographical references.
   ISBN 0–8091–3802–6 (alk. paper)
   1. Spiritual directors—Handbooks, manuals, etc. I. Title.
   BX2350.7.D58   1998
   253.5′3—dc 21   98–19893
                                               CIP

Cover design by Cynthia Dunne
Interior design by Joseph E. Petta
Typeset in 11/14 Times Roman

Published by Paulist Press
997 Macarthur Boulevard
Mahwah, New Jersey 07430

Printed and bound in the
United States of America

Contents

In loving memory of Rev. Jack Verdult, S.S.S.,
who taught me much in my young years

Preface

One might wonder what another book on spiritual direction would have to add to the vast array of books by competent authors already available in the bookstores. There are those on the Spiritual Exercises of St. Ignatius, and also some very useful and some more abstruse ones on the discernment of spirits, both Ignatian and otherwise. I have also seen various works by famous authors who have at least a dozen or more works to their name–Thomas Merton, Dr. Morton Kelsey, Fr. Thomas Green, S.J., just to name a few that come to mind immediately. So what do I feel that I have to add to these illustrious works?

I have thought about it for a while and have decided that I haven't really seen a casebook for spiritual directors. I have been going to spiritual direction for over twenty-five years, some of which was for the discernment of a celibate vocation. I finally was able to take a perpetual vow of virginity on my forty-fifth birthday in December of 1994. In the course of these twenty-five years the scenery of the church has changed quite a bit, as we all know. We have had the implementation of Vatican II, the Charismatic Renewal and Centering Prayer, which has become popular—just to name a few of the things that have taken place within my lifetime.

Also, the style of spiritual direction has changed since I started as

a teen. In my early years of spiritual direction, the director was usually a priest. What he mainly did was to encourage me to persevere
in the life of prayer, tell me I was a good girl for not fornicating like
"the others" often seemed to do and to hear my confession about
once a month. That was about the extent of spiritual direction as I
knew it in the early days of my spiritual journey. That was all in
Europe—Holland and Germany. I wasn't instructed in methods of
prayer or encouraged to read St. Teresa of Avila, St. John of the
Cross or even the Spiritual Exercises of St. Ignatius. I barely knew
that these existed and I remained ignorant of them for a long time.

When I came back to the United States at age twenty-five I found
a different approach than I had been used to with the priest directors
that were my faithful guides in my early years of Catholicism (I
became Catholic in Holland when I was eighteen in 1968). Here
direction was often given by women religious who had taken a
course of studies in spiritual direction. A more psychological
approach was taken to prayer and, of course, confessions were sepa-
rate, as the nuns couldn't hear my confession. Also different was the
emphasis on being open to everything, that is, anything that God
could want, which included marriage. I was completely floored. I
was used to thinking that because I was a young woman in spiritual
direction, my directors should have thought more in the direction of
a celibate religious vocation for me. That is what I assumed God
would want for me, as I wanted to live in close union with Jesus all
of my life. I felt that living the single or celibate life would be the
state in life that would most easily facilitate this desire.

But I found a number of directors who were telling me that
God would be close to me in *any* vocation, including married life,
as long as I did his will, whatever it was. I also had some lay
directors over the years, some of whom were married, who did
not encourage the celibate life—to put it mildly.

Finally I found a priest who was willing to work with me

toward taking private vows. I was thirty-five by that time and hurting quite a bit from all of these different direction attempts. Somehow we got through the necessary years of probation together and now I am happy to be a vowed lay woman.

For a number of years I have had people coming to me, unsolicited, for spiritual guidance and advice, as well as prayers. I have a couple of regulars who feel that I have the gift of spiritual direction, especially because I have been trying to pray since I was fourteen when I had a conversion experience, plus I have an M.A. in Christian Spirituality. Then there are my thirty articles on prayer and Christian life, which some people have said were helpful to them in their spiritual search. I have even found a number of new friends in Africa and elsewhere through the letters I've received in response to my articles published on that continent.

So I have set forth this series of case studies, which I hope will aid those looking for some references as well as insights into specific problems concerning spiritual direction. My prayers are with you as you open this book, seeking something that you can relate to. Some of the headings will look familiar: others, such as perhaps Spiritual Abuse, might be a surprise.

I hope to hear from some of you, as it is only in dialogue that we learn and grow. Let me know if anything in particular has been of special help, if you disagree with insights given under some of the entries, or if there is something you looked for but didn't find. These things can be of service to me as I perhaps will write an expanded, revised edition someday. I need your comments so that I will know which direction to go with such an endeavor.

I wish for you the Lord's blessings as you go forth on your spiritual journey, whether with someone else or alone. If you are using this book for your own spiritual growth, I accompany you in mind and spirit, knowing that the Lord will make everything clear to you through the power of his ever faithful Holy Spirit.

Introduction

I. PRELIMINARY REMARKS

It is a good sign that many people are seeking spiritual direction in our day, as this is an indication of the desire for concrete spiritual growth. With this seeking, however, comes a proliferation of spiritual directors, some of whom are better equipped than others. I have had some very sensitive, well-equipped ones, as well as some that I would rather not waste words on—of which I will mention just one. A director informed me that since I was experiencing consolation in my prayer (that is, experiencing the love of the Lord in a warm, tender way), I should try to resist these feelings. She reminded me that I could easily be deceived by the "warm fuzzies" and that I might grow slack in my prayer, and not work at it so hard. She told me to beware of those warm, tender feelings, because they would lead me astray.

You might think this sounds preposterous—that a director couldn't really say something like that. Yet it happened. And there are many similar instances I have heard about.

I am introducing this handbook with an example like this, because I want to make it clear that you should not attempt to direct people unless you have proper insight, training and ability.

This book alone is not enough. It is a "dictionary" for those who know how to cope with most situations but want to check up on a helpful way to approach some particular problem that a directee might present. It will not automatically teach you how to carry out spiritual direction and is certainly no substitute for an internship or a course of studies in spirituality or theology.

This book is also intended for those who are receiving spiritual direction, and are looking for insight into some particular spiritual problem they are dealing with. It is meant as a supplement to spiritual direction and should be used in conjunction with the guidance that the spiritual director gives in direction sessions, especially if there are any questions. Please make sure that your director is well-schooled and experienced in prayer, as this book will not help you by itself if you are not with a competent director.

Fr. Thomas Dubay explains in his work, *The Fire Within,* that there are certain criteria that a spiritual director should meet, if he or she is to be of help to us on our spiritual journey. The following is an overview of what should be looked for in a competent director, and what criteria a director should meet, if you aspire to give spiritual direction to others who come to you for help in their journey with and toward the Lord.

II. SPIRITUAL DIRECTION

St. Teresa of Avila and the Prerequisites for a Spiritual Director

To start with, a person who aspires to be a spiritual director should be well-trained. He or she need not necessarily be a priest, or religious but nevertheless ought to possess a thorough grounding in theology, especially Christian spirituality and scripture. Besides that, some knowledge of basic counseling techniques as well as familiarity with some of the more common mental problems should be present.

The need for sound theological training and experience of advanced prayer in spiritual directors was firmly insisted on by St. Teresa of Avila, one of the greatest spiritual masters of all time. Teresa herself suffered much at the hands of half-learned directors. They knew enough to think they knew it all. Some of them had no personal knowledge of advanced prayer, and thus assumed that Teresa was being proud and presumptuous when she related some of the favors that the Lord was bestowing on her. They seemed to think that because she wasn't perfect and because they had never experienced it, she couldn't possibly be going through any type of mystical experience. As a matter of fact, they even attributed her favors to the work of the devil, and forbade her to spend time in solitude, as she would then be deceived all the more.

St. Teresa was fully in accord with the biblical idea that it is foolish to trust (solely) in oneself in the area of spiritual experiences, since it is easy to be deluded or, perhaps more often, to delude oneself. St. Teresa herself, great mystic that she was, always went to her confessor-director about everything that happened in her spiritual life, even if it seemed trivial. Often, she tells us, she felt more embarrassed about her spiritual experiences and what the confessor would think of them than if she had had serious sins to confess. St. Teresa explains in her autobiography, *Life,* that the Lord told her to obey what the confessor said, even if he had said something different to her in prayer. Jesus said that he would see to it that the confessor learned the truth about whatever the disputed matter was. And true to his word in the locution, the Lord spoke to the confessor and the confessor changed his mind to line up with what the Lord had told Teresa in the locution. I find it amazing that the Lord, Teresa and the confessor were able to work this complicated interactive relationship out the way they did. Nevertheless, Teresa was humble enough not to trust her own judgment alone, but let the confessor direct her. And apparently Jesus honored this. Of course, Teresa listened to the Lord too, and didn't just blindly accept and believe everything that the confessor said. The fact that she once perceived the Lord saying that the confessor needed to change his mind says something about her humble attitude.

Choosing a Spiritual Director

What she did in her own life she advised others to do also, namely, to share experiences that she had with the Lord with her director. She took it for granted that the director was competent. Like John of the Cross, she considered him to be speaking in the name of the Lord.

a) One advantage of having a director, according to Teresa, is that a person can get advice about when to give up discursive prayer. If infused prayer is starting to grow in the interior life, a person can feel as if he or she is sort of in between. This issue can be palpably perplexing. Needless to say, if the director has little or no experience of anything beyond affective prayer, he or she won't be of much help to a person who is beginning to experience the prayer of quiet and is looking for some solid advice on how to proceed in prayer. A person who is beginning to experience the prayer of quiet may also wonder if this is real prayer, or whether he or she is being deceived and should continue discursive prayer activity. These are questions that a competent director can help to answer.

b) A second benefit flows from the first: as one is freed from the danger of illusion and from one's subjective perplexities, there arises an inner calm so helpful to contemplative growth. People who can share their prayer experiences with a competent guide find a great peace in being assured that all is well. They are then able to let go and allow the indwelling Lord to allow prayer to flow abundantly, without obstacles deriving from human fears and hesitations.

c) Once we have found a competent director to help with the

type of prayer that we are presently experiencing, it does not follow that this guide will be suitable for our needs at some other time; for an example of this one director might be knowledgable about advanced prayer, such as the prayer of quiet and the prayer of union. Another will know more about special favors like locutions and visions. Still a third one might be well versed in methods of prayer for beginners, and a fourth might be competent in the area of the psychology of religion and be able to deal with psychological difficulties in connection to prayer. St. Teresa insisted that a particular director should limit himself or herself to what he or she understands and not try to delve into areas that he or she is not familiar with. Rather, a wise and prudent director does not hesitate to refer a directee to a person in that area of competence.

St. Teresa's List of Qualities for a Spiritual Director

After all of these intimations above, we might ask what St. Teresa would look for in a spiritual director. The following are some guidelines that she gives, that which pretty much still apply today.

a) At the top of her list of desired qualities in a spiritual director was a deep and experienced prayer life as well as theological knowledge, especially in regard to the spiritual life.

Spiritual depth entails knowing advanced prayer from one's own experience, such as the prayer of quiet or maybe even the prayer of union and beyond. St. Teresa laments the fact that many spiritual directors of her day knew the prayer of quiet only from their study books, if even that much. Many had not advanced beyond affective prayer or even meditation. Ideally, a director should have inside knowledge of these stages of prayer, and if not, direct beginners only. It is common that someone who is not familiar with the prayer of quiet from his or her own experience gets anxious when somebody comes for direction who seems to be experiencing it. They give the wrong advice or simply despise the person and tell them that it is more realistic or humble to stay with discursive prayer, as advanced prayer is only for canonized saints.

b) However, if a person is experiencing the prayer of quiet for the first time and can't find anyone who possesses first-hand knowledge of this stage of prayer, it would still be helpful to consult someone who truly knows of it from studying it, such as a college professor in the area of Christian spirituality.

As St. Teresa advises, we should consult people who have studied spirituality, unless of course we have already studied it ourselves. St. Teresa did not get a chance for a college education as she was a woman, and advanced education was not customary for women back in the 1500s. Even in our day, those who don't know much about spirituality should at least read about the stages of prayer as St. Teresa presents them. Another option is to take a mini-course in spirituality such as I, and many others, give to people seeking a closer union with God. However, if we start experiencing the prayer of quiet or beyond, we then should consult a director. A book and a class usually will not be enough for those seriously committed to the practice of prayer. It seems that the devil is less able to deceive those who want to seek the truth by consulting people who know what they are talking about, or by reading about things that they are not familiar with in order to learn the truth.

c) The third quality of the director is that he or she should have a balanced view about unusual experiences in prayer. He or she should be aware that deception is possible in prayer, but also that God can and really often does deal with individual people in the life of prayer. The balanced director should realize that not every claim to hear the Spirit is really what it purports to be. On the other hand, there should be an awareness that not all grace is unperceived. St. Teresa and St. Ignatius would certainly attest to that. Ignatius often experienced consolations accompanied by great sobs. The director should also know how to distinguish deceptions from authentic experiences of God.

d) Fourth, St. Teresa points out that we shouldn't seek out a director just because he or she is likely to agree with us regarding our pet theories and will approve of all of our plans—spiritual and otherwise. Many people who pray as a "hobby," because they enjoy it, will not want to hear what a director has to say if he or she wants some discipline and consistency in the life of prayer. Some people pray only when they feel like it. They say they pray "when the Spirit inspires them," but in reality they are merely following their whims.

e) The fifth trait St. Teresa desired in a director was a genuine interest in the well-being of the directee. He or she should take a holistic approach and think of the consequences of spiritual advice on the whole structure of the individual directee's life. For instance, it doesn't do any good to recommend certain penances or prayers if they seriously interfere with the directee's work or family life. The whole picture should be seen, and the spiritual life not isolated from the rest of life.

St. John of the Cross on Spiritual Direction

St. John of the Cross emphasized Jesus as the center of the spiritual life and of spiritual direction. He believed in having a human spiritual director who would help the directee to listen to the Holy Spirit, which is the Spirit of Jesus. The Holy Spirit is the main guide; the human guide must defer to the Spirit of Jesus working within the directee.

The director is not a teacher of theological theory; rather he or she assists the directee in applying the truths of scripture and of our Catholic faith to the needs of this particular directee. Not every directee has the knowledge or ability to apply it to concrete situations. This is one area in which a competent director can provide an invaluable service.

The duties of the director are threefold according to John of the Cross. First, the director can help the directee to open himself or herself as completely as possible to the working of the Lord within. The directee needs to learn to be pliable in the hands of the Lord, without being a fall guy for other people. The director needs to realize that just because the directee needs to learn how to yield to the Lord, it doesn't mean their giving up sound judgment in the spiritual life or in other areas of life. Rather, it means their being open to listen and being willing to change their opinion if there is a good reason. Listening to the voice of God in scripture as well as to the Lord speaking to the heart should go hand in hand.

Second, the human director should also be docile to the Spirit, so that he or she will be able to listen to what the Spirit is doing in the directee. Only then will the director be able to confirm and verify from without what the Spirit seems to be doing within the directee.

Third, the human guide teaches the directee how to live according to the gospel and how to apply the word of God to everyday life. The director tries to help the directee to overcome concern with what others think, especially in regard to the directee's attempts to live the Christian life. The director should explain that it is more important to care what God thinks than what people think! The ability to instruct an individual in living the Christian life in prayer and deeds requires a thorough knowledge of scripture, mystical theology, and the teachings of the saints as well.

John's first principle, that the director should defer to the work of the Spirit in the directee and simply be a co-discerner, is complemented by the conviction that direction should also be incarnational and ecclesial.

Certainly this does not mean that a director has to be an ordained person. Many directors, if not most, are not. However, it does mean that a director ought to think with the church and direct with the eternal well-being of the directee in mind. A director cannot simply use his or her own pet theories and try them out on the directee. This is truly a kind of exploitation and must be avoided at all costs.

The Bible is replete with many examples of God communicating with his people through a particular person: Abraham, Moses, the prophets, the apostles and most of all, Mary, the mother of the Lord. One particular instance which shows that God prefers to teach people through other people, although he could have done it directly through the Spirit is in the case of Saul. Instead of filling him with the Holy Spirit on the road, Jesus instructed Saul to go into the city where he would be told what to do. Jesus himself was instructed in human and religious customs by his mother, Mary. The Word Incarnate had to learn from his mother and father the most basic things which made him fully human.

In the spiritual life God does sometimes lead a person through locutions, visions and intuitions, but even then he often wants the directee to have the message confirmed by a spiritual director. This person serves as a co-discerner and fellow journeyer.

St. John's Guidelines for Spiritual Directors

St. John of the Cross, too, has his guidelines for a spiritual director. They are similar to Teresa's in that he feels the director should be learned, sensitive and discreet and have experience in the life of prayer. By "discretion" John means that a director should possess good, sound judgment, especially in regard to applying the general principles of spirituality to the person's individual case. By "discretion" he also envisions a sound knowledge of practical human psychology.

Faults in a Spiritual Director

John hates to see directees abused. I dwell on this issue as well, which will be obvious as you read through the pages of the text. He could really use strong language when it came to spiritual mistreatment on the part of incompetent directors. Here are some of the points that he makes in his writings regarding this problem:

a) The first defect he points to is attempting to lead those who are advanced in prayer along the way of beginners. Some directors are knowledgeable of meditation only, even though they may have been priests or religious for many years. They seem to think that anybody who claims to be further along than meditation is arrogant and out of line. They hasten to explain to the poor directee that one cannot become lazy in prayer and just sit there. Rather, they should get a new meditation book and work harder at it. This is completely contrary to what the Lord would want. They are bungling what God is trying to accomplish. The results can be disastrous for the directee spiritually, and maybe even psychologically.

b) St. John characterizes the second mistake of incompetent directors as that of misinterpreting ordinary human sufferings as the dark night of the soul. I don't mean to minimize common human suffering, and I don't think that John meant to either. However, the director who labels every suffering "the dark night of the soul" has not understood what is meant by the term in mystical theology, and thus can hinder, rather than help, one who is truly experiencing this particular trial in prayer.

c) The third fault is to cling to one's directee and to try to prevent him or her from seeking help from someone who knows more about what is presently going on in their prayer life than the present director does. John doesn't expect one director to be adequate for all the needs of a spiritually growing directee. For one who is stagnant it might be another matter, although for such a one, it might be good to hear another point of view from a new director.

Otherwise, the directee whose spiritual growth has slowed down can completely fall asleep.

d) St. John saved the most searing label for a lax guide: he or she is truly pestiferous. This can be a real problem for a beginner who is trying to grow in prayer and is very fervent. The tepid director can really discourage a person who wants to advance spiritually from trying at all any more, just by his or her human rationalizations and lukewarmness.

III. SPIRITUAL DIRECTION AND PASTORAL COUNSELING

Finally, I would like to present a couple of brief thoughts on spiritual direction and pastoral counseling. Most of the entries in this book are strictly of the spiritual-direction type. They deal with prayer and its stages, and problems that can arise in the course of the journey with the Lord. Included in this category are headings that deal with consolation with previous cause, the presence of God, mansions, being born again, pettiness in doing God's will, and alternating spirits, as well as many others.

On the other hand, there are entries that tend to fall more into the pastoral counseling category, such as absolution, suicide, and the like. These entries deal with emotional problems and similar personal crises.

So what is the difference between the two? Obviously, they are interrelated. As a rule of thumb, the spiritual direction category deals with one's relationship to God and the life of prayer as such. A spiritual director should be able to help with this area of concern by teaching about types of prayer, discernment, and so forth. More than anything else, a director should be a fellow-journeyer, a co-discerner. It should be someone who knows about prayer from personal experience, and is able to guide someone who is making the spiritual journey to God.

A spiritual director should ideally have some theological background, with a concentration in Christian spirituality. Hopefully, he or she will have also done an internship in spiritual direction. These are the minimum prerequisites for a person desiring to serve as a spiritual director to others. A spiritual director should always be willing to learn more and love learning more about his or her faith. That in addition to a consistent life with the church, which may include daily mass, and certainly daily silent prayer and spiritual reading.

A pastoral counselor will deal with emotional problems and adjustment difficulties that aren't too serious, and which don't require the services of a licensed therapist or clinical psychologist or even a psychiatrist. These difficulties will be put under the spotlight of our Catholic Christian faith. People who come to a pastoral counselor often, if not always, desire that the problems they are dealing with be worked on from the perspective and message of the gospel of Jesus and the Catholic Church. The problems may be marriage problems, family problems, work-related tensions, anxiety and depression, to name but a few. Pastoral counselors can also help deal with mid-life crisis situations, and pre-marital counseling. They focus not so much on hearing the Lord in the person, as in hearing the person. They try to work with the person and his or her salient or underlying problems from a perspective of Christian faith.

Spiritual direction attempts to help the directee listen to the Lord who is working within him or her, especially in the life of prayer. Pastoral counseling tries to aid the counselee in finding visable (if possible, Christian) solutions to problems dealt with in everyday life. As you can see, the two overlap, yet are different in their approach and emphasis.

A pastoral counselor is hopefully a person with a background in theology, but also in pastoral counseling, perhaps through a pastoral counseling institute, or maybe with a masters in social work or in counseling. A counselor should also be a person of faith, but the psychological training is a must. Many pastoral counselors tend to be priests, deacons and pastoral associates in the parish setting. They often encounter people who need some pastoral counseling in the course of sacramental preparation, a death in the family and so forth.

IV. CONCLUSION

With these thoughts, admonitions and warnings in mind, I wish you success in finding the entries in the following pages helpful for issues in spiritual direction. The pastoral counseling entries have been included to make you aware of some of the issues that can come up during direction that should be referred to competent pastoral counselors, if you are not equipped to handle them yourself. It is better to refer too often, than not do it enough. We shouldn't be ashamed to admit that the needs of some people are beyond our abilities to help. The welfare of the directee should always take precedence over our desire to handle the needs of all.

Handbook of Definitions

Absolution

Difficulties presented: Fully distressed, Sally comes to you. She explains that she had an abortion because her child was illegitimate, and the father pressured her into it. She has since then had remorse about the act of abortion, went to confession, received absolution and had her excommunication lifted. Yet she wonders if forgiveness took place as she doesn't feel forgiven. What would you suggest in order to aid this soul full of anguish?

Underlying meaning: Sally needs to be aware of the fact that a deeper healing will probably need to take place, which can possibly be accomplished by seeing a compassionate pastoral counselor. She needs to be reassured that God's forgiveness really was given in the sacrament of reconciliation as God never refuses forgiveness to people who are sorry for their sins. He promises to forgive us in Jesus Christ as many scripture passages attest. If there is an issue of feeling unloved or unworthy that remains from past years, perhaps professional help should be sought.

Suggestions: Praying with Sally to be able to know and accept God's love and forgiveness in a felt way might be good. Sally should also be told that even if the feeling doesn't come, that she can accept the forgiveness in faith. Perhaps the director could also

pray for Sally to be able to forgive herself. Something that is difficult to deal with is when the person has offended someone, has
asked for forgiveness and the forgiveness has been refused, or
when public scandal has been given by some sin. In these cases,
continued prayer with and for the individual, as well as professional counseling, is recommended so that the person can learn to
accept herself without the approval of the other person or people
in general, whatever the case may be.

Alternating Spirits

Difficulties presented: The directee, Philip, asks for advice on
what to do about some confusing feelings in prayer. He is feeling
a lot of different spiritual and perhaps other vibes and is asking
the Lord for guidance on what to do about taking a new job. On
one hand, he feels that this would be a promotion for him, but it
would give him less time for his family, as he would often have to
work extra hours. In the new job he would be able to witness more
effectively to his faith; the shadow side would be less financial
security. He is asking the Lord for guidance, but doesn't seem to
get any clear message. It seems to be both. What would you tell
this confused person?

Underlying meaning: It often seems that with alternating
spirits, God wants to bestow a gift or have a person do something,
but wants to leave the person his freedom. Sometimes it may
involve a decision that God is leaving up to the recipient of the
alternating spirits. It could be that the time for the decision to be
made has not arrived yet, because not all of the facts, that is, the
consequences of the alternatives, are known to the directee or the
director or both. Also, sometimes the time isn't ripe yet, and the
person needs to grow and to be more mature in order to be able to
respond in an appropriate way.

Suggestions: Encourage Philip to make a list of the pros and
cons of each aspect of the decision and to bring them before the

Lord in prayer. Ask Philip to try to listen to the Lord and to his own heart and see where he feels most encouraged, and what makes him feel despondent. Have him discuss the results of bringing the pros and cons of the decision to be made with you as the director, and pray with him to have peace about whatever decision is made. If possible, have Philip do a trial run with the decision; that is, if the circumstances permit, have him try out the decision to see if it works in his life.

Angel of Light

Difficulties presented: The directee, Denise, explains that she has been having experiences of light and illumination in her prayer and feels good while she is having these feelings, but feels depressed, discouraged and disillusioned after they leave. She wonders why she is getting sad and discouraged if the Lord is giving her consolations. She also wonders what she should do in response to these experiences of light and insight. Should she follow the vibes or not? What would you tell her in this instance?

Underlying meaning: The angel of light is the evil spirit, the devil. The evil spirit can give false consolation. It seems like the Lord is giving a certain inspiration or illumination, but it makes us sad and falls to shreds when it is acknowledged for what it is. The best way to discern a true from a false consolation is the type of effect it has on us. If it seems to draw us closer to God, gives us a desire to grow in holiness—that is, grow in God's ways—it probably is from the Lord. If it seems to give us good ideas, but leads nowhere and serves to make us feel proud and self-satisfied, it probably is from the angel of light; that is, it is a false consolation (Cf. Rules for the Discernment of Spirits in the writings of St. Ignatius of Loyola).

Suggestions: It takes experience to discern true from false consolations in the beginning of the spiritual life as well as later on. Especially since Denise practices interior prayer on a regular basis, it is good to consult a person experienced in the ways of prayer, someone who has had experience in sorting out spiritual events, and hopefully also has some background study in Christian spirituality. It is also helpful to keep a spiritual journal, especially highlighting experiences of consolation and desolation as they appear on the scene of our life of prayer. As we persevere in this discipline of journal writing, we will begin to discern the Lord's influence from the angel of light—especially as we read over what we have written and sort out the good from the bad; that is, compare different experiences that we have had and draw the appropriate conclusions.

Anger with God

Difficulties presented: Scott comes for spiritual direction, furious with God because of the death of his doting mother, as well as some other misfortunes like job loss, resulting in loss of income, abandonment by many friends, etc. Scott asks what he should do for things to get better again.

Underlying meaning: It is understandable that a person can become angry with God, as people figure that's where the buck stops. However, our suffering is not God's fault, something that he causes, although he does permit it. But we don't always know the reason for it. However suffering, if it cannot be alleviated, can be offered up and united with the suffering of Christ and thus be sanctifying, both for our salvation as well as that of other people. St. Paul tells us that he is crucified with Christ and that his sufferings make up for what is lacking in the sufferings of Christ for the sake of his body, the church.

However, in the meantime, Scott is angry.

Suggestions: The best thing to do is to admit this anger to God and oneself and not try to hide or deny the hurt, which is very real. However, we shouldn't stay at that stage if we want to grow spiritually and allow our relationship to God to be healed. If Scott talks to a spiritual director about the hurt, reads in scripture about the healing power of Jesus, as well as some other helpful scripture passages, he might be able to find meaning in his suffering, even if it cannot be alleviated immediately. Also, writing about his feelings in a journal, and perhaps writing some letters to God in his journal, telling God how he feels and asking him to feel his hurt with him and to heal his affliction can work wonders. Some people who are especially distressed find it helpful to draw or paint pictures concerning their pain as a means of getting it out of their system. If all of this doesn't seem to help or help enough, Scott might need to be referred for professional counseling.

Angry at God

Difficulties presented: Mary is angry with God because of the injustice in the world and because she feels that God looks on and does nothing. She just had her savings wiped out by an unreliable bank, had to borrow money to go to school, had unfair teachers who made her grades lower than they should have been, and as a consequence has been unable to get a job that pays enough money to liquidate the student loans and to build up her savings again.

Her language is somewhat vulgar as the predicament is described. She dares you to answer for God as you are seen as his representative. How could you dare be on the side of a God who allows so much misery in the world, especially her own painful experiences? What can you do in a situation like this one?

Underlying meaning: Since there are so many injustices in the world, it is not easy to give a straightforward answer to this one. These questions have baffled people for years and years, especially since the Enlightenment, when people began to hold God accountable for what he was doing in their lives. One thing that is recommended is to try not to be too defensive of oneself as a religious person, or of God, as if he needed to be defended.

Suggestions: It might be good to just listen to Mary in an active listening mode and to try to be supportive of her personal pain. A person usually doesn't get so angry unless there is an underlying reason. When Mary is finished expressing her anger, and letting it all out, an attempt can be made to explain the free will of the human person, that is, for good or for evil, as well as the fact that God suffers with us in this broken world in Jesus Christ. And that, finally, we don't know all the answers, but that God asks for us to have a stance of faith, which is a gift, and to help him to work to make this world a better place to live.

Antagonism from Peers

Difficulties presented: Agnes is almost in tears. She has begun to be a religious person, that is, has begun the practice of regular prayer and sometimes daily mass. All of a sudden those who are closest to her are making snide remarks and are trying to dissuade her from these "exaggerated religious practices," or "religious fanaticism." What should Agnes be told in regard to this type of harassment?

Underlying meaning: This problem is more common than we would think, but a solution is not always easy to find. It seems that if we really take God and our faith seriously, we will offend some people that we thought were our friends, just as many people in Jesus' time liked his healing people, although some didn't because he healed on the sabbath. Yet when he taught that he was the Son of God, a lot of people decided that was going too far and wanted to kill him. In the Acts of the Apostles the disciples felt that it was a privilege to be counted worthy to suffer for Jesus' sake, but most of us don't usually have the courage for that stance. But that is sometimes what we are called to do—to stand up and be counted.

Suggestions: Things to do would be to relate the above to Agnes and explain that it is a privilege to be ridiculed, which is a mild form of suffering, for Jesus' sake. Agnes can be encouraged to pray for her friends, to try to explain in a tactful way why she is practicing the faith this way now. If they do not relent, she should try to find supportive friends, all the while praying for the ones that are making fun of her. If need be, Agnes can pray privately or with the director for the ability to forgive these friends for their shortsightedness.

Boredom in Prayer

Difficulties presented: John comes for direction. He is a committed religious person and has had a fervent spiritual awakening, but now his relationship to Jesus seems to be on the rocks. John has asked the Lord to manifest to him his love and concern, but seemingly to no avail. He feels that God has turned a deaf ear. His prayer is now very boring and he has had many temptations to give up, because he feels that God, who gave him a spiritual awakening, has cheated him and let him down. He wonders whether this boredom will persist for the rest of his life, and if so, whether the boredom is worth weathering.

Underlying meaning: In life it is simply not possible to sustain a bubbly feeling, whether it be in religious experience or in other areas of concern. Life just has many everyday aspects and the life of prayer is no exception. It is not expected that this boredom will last for the rest of our lives, providing that we do the necessary things to sustain and nourish our relationship to the Lord.

Suggestions: Things to do include the reading and reflection on scripture, especially the gospels; receiving the sacraments; praying in spite of boredom —although sometimes it might be good to change some of our prayer practices. We might change the position of our body when we pray, maybe the time when we pray, the kind of prayer that we perform (such as vocal prayer instead of silent prayer), etc. It is good to try different things to see what works for us, just like we might try different things in our relationship to a spouse or friend, just in order to please him or her.

Born Again

Difficulties presented: Jo Ann comes to you saying that she has been born again and wonders whether you are "saved" too. She feels that many of her fellow parishioners don't know the riches of God's love which are manifested when we are born again, and she wants them to know the fullness of the joy of the Lord. Jo Ann wants to start a campaign to get all of her fellow parishioners saved and wants to enlist your help. How would you respond?

Underlying meaning: According to Catholic theology, we are saved as a community. As we believe in Jesus and his message and try to live out the gospel with the help of his grace, which includes participation in the life of the church, the community of believers, we are saved. Catholics believe that salvation is a process, not just a one-time event. To be "saved" in this particular manner is more of an evangelical Protestant concept and doesn't fit in with Catholic theology. It still might be good to belong to a charismatic prayer group and be baptized in the Holy Spirit, if a person feels some benefit is to be gained from this. However, eternal salvation shouldn't have to depend on belonging to a charismatic prayer group, although it can be an aid along the way.

Suggestions: Explain your viewpoint to Jo Ann, which is elaborated above, if that is your viewpoint. Help her to realize that in a Catholic parish it is not right or feasible to try to get everybody to have the same experience that she claims to have had of being born again, even though it might help, especially if it proves to bear fruit, the fruit spoken of in Galatians 5: love, peace, joy.

Centering Prayer

Difficulties presented: Ruth finds that she is beginning to pray deeper and is having a pleasant experience of the presence of the Lord. She enjoys it and starts to relax and surrender to the Lord, telling him that she wants more of this, and that she wishes she had

had this experience earlier in life. She wonders whether this is legitimate prayer or whether it is prayer at all, as she doesn't seem to be doing anything and she feels that she needs to do something in order to be praying. Although she enjoys this prayer, she feels guilty about the passivity. How would you advise her as her director?

Underlying meaning: Centering prayer has a long tradition in Christianity, even though some these days would try to discount it and want to make all prayer active. Of course there are certain pitfalls, if you want to call them that, like getting in touch with repressed psychological conflicts, with unfinished business and unhealed memories. If need be, a person who gets in touch with these types of problems through the practice of centering prayer might want to go for psychotherapy, all the while asking the Lord Jesus to be Lord of her unconscious mind and to heal the emotional pain which makes it difficult to continue in prayer.

Suggestions: Ruth might want to keep a journal and record what types of difficulties come up in the practice of prayer, whether they are emotional hurts with other people, bad dreams, hurts or disappointments with God himself—like resentment about unanswered prayer, etc. These things can be presented to the director and/or therapist and talked and/or prayed about. The Lord can be asked to show Ruth those who need to be forgiven in her life, as well as where the Lord and Ruth need to affirm and nurture her(self) so she can be healed.

Confidentiality

Difficulties presented: Beverly comes to you distraught because a person in her charismatic prayer group, who purports to have the gifts of the Holy Spirit, is using them to discern things about Beverly's past life. Beverly was a little promiscuous and did some other things that she is now ashamed of and has repented for. She wonders how God can permit this sister in the Lord, who is supposed to be a loving, supportive person, to disclose the secrets of her heart to other people. She feels that these people now despise her. Beverly thought that when she confessed her sins to the priest in the sacrament of reconciliation what she said would stay there. She is flabbergasted that so-called Christian people are spreading her past life out for all to see. What would you do to help Beverly? She thought that God had sovereign control over these gifts and wouldn't permit things like this to come to light.

Underlying meaning: It can be quite shocking to find that there are people that have the gift of reading the hearts of others, especially your own, but downright devastating to realize that the person with the gift is not using love and discretion when exercising this gift. There are people who have experienced this, and it is really a violation of privacy. There are some things that only the confessor should know, and other things that perhaps we only dare to tell the Lord.

There is no ready-made answer as to why God permits this type of abuse of the gifts of the Holy Spirit except that he respects our human freedom, and permits the abuse of many other good gifts as well: sex, money, power, etc., which can all be good things if used for the glorification of God and for the good of other people.

Suggestions: A suggestion is that Beverly let go of the person or group of people that is practicing this type of abuse because that is what it is—real spiritual and psychological abuse. She should stay away and not let herself be coaxed into coming back under any condition. In the meantime, the director could try to support Beverly emotionally and explain that any or all gifts can be abused and that God will take care of it in his time. Our duty is to cherish ourselves as the Lord does and to pray to be free from the pain and disappointment in these brothers and sisters in the Lord. We should also try to forgive them with the help of the Lord's grace, and, if appropriate, warn other people who might get hurt. If Beverly can't get over the pain and shock of the betrayal by your efforts as a spiritual director, you may have to refer her for pastoral or professional counseling.

Confusion about God's Will

Difficulties presented: Jane comes to you, saying that she isn't sure what God's will is about giving up her job and taking early retirement in order to help her elderly mother and father. She has prayed for guidance from the Lord, but seems to get no clear sense of what to do. On the contrary, she just gets more confused, the more she prays. She is nearly at her wit's end, trying to figure out what God could want in this situation. She also is afraid that if she chooses the wrong thing, that God won't protect her and love her anymore. She is afraid of being out of his will and of forfeiting his care and protection in her life. How would you try to help Jane in her perplexity?

Underlying meaning: For a Christian it is important to try to do God's perceived will in every circumstance of life. Some people tend to think that discernment of God's will is only appropriate when a person has to discern whether to become a priest or religious, or if and whom to marry. They don't seem to realize that discernment is a way of life, a way of allowing God to be involved in every aspect of one's daily life.

For small matters, a rigorous discernment process is not required. For more important matters, more prayer and weighing of the possible consequences of the decision should be undertaken. For weighty decisions, there are various schools of discernment from which to draw. One popular one is that of St. Ignatius with his rules for the discernment of spirits. There are also others, like St. Teresa of Avila's rules for the discernment of locutions and visions—to be found in her *Life* as well as in her *Interior Castle* (Life 25; Interior Castle VI:3:1).

Suggestions: For small matters it should be sufficient to do whatever keeps one on the path to God and doesn't cause too much friction in our relationship with the Lord. Of course this presupposes a felt and experienced relationship in frequent, and if possible, daily prayer. If we pray to be in conformity with God's will in our daily life, we will intuitively sense what is most pleasing to him, what enables us to live in peace with the Lord. Perhaps Jane can write down the pros and cons and present them to the Lord in a journal, asking him as a spouse to show what would be most pleasing to him. Often it seems that prayer is like a relationship between a husband and wife who have been married for many years and more or less know the likes and dislikes, the thoughts and desires of the other without having to be told.

Consolation with Previous Cause

Difficulties presented: Joe, the directee, is experiencing what we would call consolation with previous cause (Cf. Ignatius: Rules for Discernment). That is to say, Joe has been doing some spiritual reading and has been experiencing consolation from the Lord as he gets into the text and reflects on it. This is the most common form of divine consolation. It consists in feelings of illuminating insights, warm feelings of being loved by the Lord, an increased hunger for prayer, etc. This type of consolation has its origin in something that we as praying people do to open ourselves to receiving consolation from the Lord. This is in contrast to the spontaneous consolation, also called consolation without previous cause, where nothing that we directly did brought on the consolation; also consolation without previous cause is out of all proportion to our expectations and to anything we possibly could have done to bring it upon ourselves.

Underlying meaning: We might have been doing meditative reading when something strikes us as being a message from the Lord for us. This would be a good example of consolation with previous cause, as the meditation on scripture, or some other spiritual book, gave us the openness to receive an insight from the

Lord which can be called a consolation, since it is something that leads us closer to the Lord. Another instance of consolation with previous cause might be the hearing of good music and feeling close to God as a result of this experience. It can also be attending mass, or meeting a certain person who encourages or challenges us. It can be any number of things, like watching a sunset or walking on a beach. It is true that God gives the consolation, that is, the awareness of his presence and his love, but something created opened us up to the receiving of this grace. There is a proportion between the means and the consolation itself.

Suggestions: Rejoice with Joe that God is making himself felt through the consolations which are being given. Help Joe to learn to distinguish those that are of the Lord and those that perhaps stem more from purely human desire—that is, wishful thinking—not to speak of the enemy of our nature. Consider whether a consolation makes Joe want to praise and be close to the Lord and to love him and other people, or whether the consolation makes him more wrapped up in himself and all too aware of how "special" he is in contrast to other people. See also the guidelines for discernment of locutions under the heading Locutions.

Consolation without Previous Cause

Difficulties presented: Sue has been having some very striking experiences of the Lord without much preparation for it. She has been a Christian for a long time but has never really experienced anything quite like this. She wonders what the meaning of this is, because a lot of light and warmth is being experienced, as well as sometimes strong impressions that God is speaking to her mind. The directee also wonders if there is anything in particular that she should be doing as a response to these graces. How would you explain this situation to the directee?

Underlying meaning: The term consolation without previous cause stems from the works of St. Ignatius of Loyola in his section on the discernment of spirits. Briefly, consolation without previous cause is a consolation from God, which has no prior human preparation as its source, such as meditation, attending mass, being comforted by the words of a friend, etc. It is an encounter with the living God that comes out of the blue, so to speak, without our expecting it or being able to control its coming and going, its strength or type. A good example of a consolation without previous cause would be the encounter of Paul with Jesus on the road to Damascus (Acts 9), the coming of the angel Gabriel to the Virgin Mary (Lk 1:26-38) or the resurrection appearances of Jesus to his disciples (Lk 24; Jn 20-21). A consolation without previous cause is disproportionate to what we expect and to any effort we ever could possibly put forth. It is something that God initiates and we have only to receive. It seems that the graces of the prayer of union in all of its stages (*Interior Castle* IV-VII), which St. Teresa so vividly describes, are examples of consolation without previous cause, because no amount of preparation can make it happen. Preparation can only open us to receive, but not bring about, divine favors and encounters.

Suggestions: The most important thing is to be open to the working of God through the power of his Holy Spirit as best we can with the help of God's grace. Some spiritual traditions advise us not to ask God for special favors and some say that it is okay to ask the Lord to allow us to encounter him. It is good to keep in mind, whatever school of thought we follow, to keep our eyes on the Giver of the warmth, light or whatever we experience, and not on the gift. This is a grace that we need to ask for, as it is difficult not to want these exalted gifts that the Lord bestows on his beloved people. To realize that he is so much greater than all of his gifts and to adore him whether or not we experience anything is probably an even greater gift. Nevertheless, we should be grateful when the Lord bestows consolations without previous cause, as he must think we need them. Otherwise he would not give them to us. Who are we to say that we don't need what the Lord wants to give us?

Consolations

Difficulties presented: A young, devout, single woman named Nancy is experiencing strong consolations in her prayer, which are experienced like warmth and light, sometimes even caresses from the Lord. She feels strongly attracted to prayer and wants to live all of her life with the Lord. She wants to make sure that she is really experiencing the Lord in her prayer, and that she is not going astray, so asks for guidance in discerning these experiences of light and warmth. She wants to make sure that it is really Jesus that she is encountering and not some figment of her imagination. She also wants to know how she can worthily respond to the Lord who is revealing himself so lovingly to her.

Underlying meaning: God often gives consolations to young people as well as older ones, to encourage them to commit themselves to him and to draw them to a lifetime of prayer and service to him and his people. God presents himself as the divine bridegroom, as he is depicted in scripture (Is 62:4-5) as well as in Catholic tradition in the experience of some of the saints (St. Teresa of Avila, St. Therese of Lisieux, St. Catherine of Siena, St. Bernard of Clairvaux, St. John of the Cross, to name but a few). This is a time of great graces and should be enjoyed gratefully and responded to generously as it seems to prepare for times of dryness and trials later in the spiritual journey.

Suggestions: Nancy ought to thank the Lord for his special love and ask him to allow her to be faithful to him, even when these particular favors are not being experienced. She should allow his love to permeate the woundedness of her inner child, so that she can truly be an adult lover of the Lord and of other people. God might want to give Nancy some special gift for the church, like a celibate religious vocation. If so, she might want to ask the Lord for guidance and for the generosity to follow this calling, if it is his will. The Lord invites; he usually does not compel, but we do well to follow his persistent leading because he knows what is best for us.

Consolations, Not Seeking

Difficulties presented: Peggy is enjoying prayer after having struggled to make the commitment to regular prayer time. She now prays about half an hour in the morning and half an hour in the evening. However, she is getting attached to the warmth and light and other nice feelings that accompany prayer to the extent that she does not want to do her other duties as they ought to be performed. Instead, she would rather spend the whole day in prayer and enjoy these nice insights, illuminations, etc. She is starting to hear the Lord call her to action, that is, to share with others the gifts that she has received in prayer from the Lord. However, she is unsure how to go about it. She feels that she doesn't know how to communicate her favors to other people, and besides that they are quite personal and inappropriate to share with others. What would you advise?

Underlying meaning: It is truly a great grace to be consoled by the Lord and, besides that, to be willing to set other things aside in order to receive this experience of his love in prayer. The Lord knows that we need to receive his favors in order to become weaned from being too attached to the purely worldly and natural things in life. As good as they may be, sometimes they keep us from being closer to the Lord and from seeking him and his kingdom first (Mt 6:33), for our first allegiance should always be to the Lord. However, if the consolations are becoming a problem, and are keeping a person from performing everyday duties, it may be wise to exhort the directee not to be overly attached to consolations. We should pray to seek the Lord, who is the God of all consolations, and not go to prayer just to receive his consolations.

That is what St. John of the Cross would call spiritual gluttony and that is clearly an excess. We should try to keep a balance in our lives and ask for the grace to seek God for his own sake in everything in life, including our daily duties and not just in prayer, even if it is especially consoling.

Also, if the person has a particularly hard time with being overly attached to consolations, she should ask herself if some therapy might be needed for problems with low self-esteem and related things, as perhaps the consolations are filling a void that should be taken care of by psychological healing from other sources. However, many times the Lord gives consolations that is, experiences of his acceptance and love, in order to heal a wounded person. We should use discretion in telling a person to go to therapy, as it is possible the Lord will give the person the healing needed through his warmth and acceptance in prayer. Normally, it seems, some of both may be needed.

Suggestions: Advise Peggy to try to seek God for his own sake, that is, to seek the Lord, no matter what type of experience comes into awareness during prayer. It is okay to accept the consolations of the Lord and to enjoy them thoroughly if he bestows them. He gives them because he wants to draw us to himself and to bind us with cords of love. He wants us to be bonded with him as a child is with its mother. However, if the Lord withdraws the consolation, this doesn't mean that he doesn't love us anymore. Perhaps he wants to strengthen our faith so that we can follow him faithfully, no matter what we are feeling. If Peggy is having trouble with the withdrawal of consolations, maybe she could keep a journal about this and find some catharsis.

Deception during Spiritual Consolation

Difficulties presented: Meghan is having consolations; that is, feelings of light and warmth and interesting insights in her prayer, which make her quite happy. However, they seem to be leading nowhere. When the prayer is over, she feels like things are harder and dryer and feels disinclined to live for the Lord, instead of being consoled and strengthened to give herself to the Lord's service. What would you suggest?

Underlying meaning: It is quite possible to be deceived by the evil spirit in our prayer (St. Ignatius: Rules for Discernment), especially if we are practicing prayer for the lift that we get out of it, or in order to say that we practice prayer. If a lot of self-seeking is involved in the practice of prayer, it is easy to be deceived, and it is possible to receive so-called false consolations.

However, we should be aware that this is not the only reason that we may be having hard and dry times, and are perhaps even experiencing rebellious feelings against God outside of, or even during, prayer. As Dr. Gerald May explains in his works on psychiatry and spiritual direction, often after a person has had a particularly deep and illuminating experience of the Lord and has given herself to his love, the ego wants to assert its independence again. He explains that the ego of the person feels threatened by the surrender to God and immersion in him and wants to be her own person. We can assume that God understands that and doesn't expect us to surrender completely all at once. As we grow in the spiritual life and in trust and communion with the Lord, we will want to give ourselves more fully to him. He doesn't force us, but is patient and waits until we are ready.

Suggestions: Ask Meghan about the course of the consolation. It is advisable to notice whether the consolation is leading us toward God in the beginning, middle and end. Very often a consolation seems to be leading us toward the Lord, but then it goes off on a tangent somewhere along the way. Thus the middle and/or the end could be stemming from our all too human desires and/or the devil. Thus, we can, with the help of the guidelines of St. Ignatius, consider whether a consolation is leading us all the way to the Lord or whether it is veering off somewhere, leading elsewhere. Meghan can then be advised to act accordingly, and either accept it as being from the Lord or rebuke and reject it in the name of Jesus.

Desert Experience in Prayer

Difficulties presented: Jim comes to you for help as a spiritual director because he is utterly at a loss as to what has happened in his prayer life. He was enjoying warmth, refreshment and good feelings in prayer. Gradually he became aware of these good feelings dissipating, leaving him with a taste of sawdust in the mouth. Jim is distressed, wondering if he has offended God and that God therefore has abandoned him for his lukewarmness or sins. He points out that God led his people from Israel through the desert for forty years for their disobedience and unbelief and stubbornness. He wonders if that is what is happening to him. He is feeling a lot of remorse about past sins and is fearful that this prayer experience is an indication that God doesn't want him to be with him in heaven. How would you as a director deal with this situation that Jim is in?

Underlying meaning: It seems that this is a fairly common experience, even though it is not pleasant. Jim feels that springtime arrived with a spiritual awakening, and then all of a sudden he felt lost, in the middle of nowhere. It is important to realize that if we are being conscientious in our prayer and Christian life, we are not backsliding, but rather going forward. We are being led toward a newer and deeper knowledge of the Lord and his love for us. It is easy to say that we should rejoice, but we really should be happy that God is continuing the journey with us. Some have said that we are letting go of more sensory communications and becoming accommodated to more spiritual communications of the Lord. St. John of the Cross explains that after we have sucked fully from the breast of the mother, which is God, she puts us down, and teaches us to walk on our own two feet. So this is not a reason to be discouraged, but to be happy.

Suggestions: In this situation it would be good to just try to be quiet and wait on the Lord in prayer. It isn't necessary to always be doing or even experiencing something in prayer in order for it to be worthwhile. We can just let God work at a deeper level. Eventually God's presence is all that really matters; we are "wasting" time with him. We can read some scripture from time to time and try to talk to the Lord about it, if that works too.

Desolation

Difficulties presented: Bruce is having a very hard time persevering in prayer. In fact, all kinds of fears, temptations, and locutions that are confusing to him (and thus probably false) abound. Bruce is about to give up. It seems that God has forsaken him, yet he is aware that this may be a tactic of the devil to make him discouraged about prayer and the things of God. The very thought that the evil one is tempting him scares him, yet he wants to be on God's side, so he seeks advice on how to proceed. How would you counsel this individual?

Underlying meaning: St. Ignatius speaks of desolation in his Spiritual Exercises; it can be difficulties and discouragement in prayer as well as false consolations (such as the locutions mentioned above). Desolation is anything that takes the individual away from God and the things of his kingdom. Desolation can be difficult to endure, precisely because it wears on us where we are weakest. It can wear on our nerves and our health in general, if we don't entrust ourselves to God and let him take care of what is going on. In spite of the remorse, scruples, fears, doubts, anxiety or perhaps a false sense of elation, it is possible to abandon ourselves to God's mercy and care, and surrender in blind faith. God in his time will remove the trial, or if not, will give us the strength to endure what we are going through, because he is faithful and will not let us be tried beyond our strength (1 Cor 10:13).

Suggestions: Trying to relax and to see that God's love is allowing us to be tried in order to make us more dependent on him and his love is the best strategy. Bruce, in this situation, should attempt not to take himself too seriously and realize that God is still in control, even though it seems that he is uninvolved with Bruce in his neediness. Of course this experience of desolation is a hard blow to our pride, as we might have practiced prayer for years by this time and thought that we were beyond the types of fears, doubts and temptations that present themselves to us. But it is precisely in this situation that God allows us to feel our weakness and to die to self so as to live more fully in and for him. Explaining all of this to Bruce seems to be the best strategy, as is encouraging him to persevere in spite of trials.

Detachment

Difficulties presented: Bob, who is very devout, and wants to be pleasing to the Lord in everything, asks for advice on how frugally he should live. Bob wants to be poor like Jesus, but also wants to be able to do justice to his family and work. How would you discuss this with Bob?

Underlying meaning: Evangelical poverty is one of the evangelical counsels that nuns and order priests and brothers vow to live. It is recommended, but not mandatory, that all Christians in light of the world situation—with so many poor and hungry people, both in our country as well as in others—not use more than they really need. However, not everybody is called to live evangelical poverty. We all are called, though, to be responsible stewards of God's gifts of finances, as well as other gifts, and to share with those who have less than we do. Jesus' admonition in Matthew 25, where he judges everyone according to what they did for the least of his brethren, is often not taken seriously enough.

Suggestions: Explain this concept of evangelical poverty and the call of stewardship to Bob. Tell him that he can try to live more frugally in his personal life, but that it might not be easy or perhaps even advisable to try to impose this frugality on all of his family. It has to be a free choice, a response to God's call on the part of each family member individually. It might be good to encourage young children to share their allowance or other things with those who have less, to teach them that not all children in the world have what they have been blessed with. Learning this at a young age will hopefully help later attitudes to be more Christian in this area of life.

Doubts

Difficulties presented: Bill, who identifies himself as a skeptic, comes for direction and guidance, asking whether we can know that there is a God. He has been trying to pray, but wonders whether his prayer life is based on illusion, and whether the so-called experiences that he is having in prayer are figments of his imagination. He is quite an intellectual person who feels that faith should be based on something besides feelings, like human reason. How would you respond?

Underlying meaning: Doubts can stem from a number of different sources, some of which are secularism, bad example, personal conflicts of growth, and self-deception. Then there is angry doubt which can arise from depression, anxiety, or both. Often persons who are depressed and anxious about loss of faith will feel angry at God whom they think has caused or allowed something bad to happen to them. Finally, there is the arrogance of the intellect that may arise from human knowledge which is used inappropriately, just as free will can be used the wrong way (Cf. Benedict Groeschel, *Stumbling Blocks or Stepping Stones,* chapter 2).

Suggestions: (1) Recognize that Bill is having doubts. (2) Ask yourself what is at the bottom of the doubt. Has Bill been influenced by the spirit of the world? Has Bill accepted the fallacies of modern philosophy? Maybe it all stems from a spirit of unbelief, or he could be anxious or frustrated.

Perhaps Bill has been trying to escape the cross in life and did not want to accept suffering when it came. It could be that Bill is angry with teachers or parents or other significant people and is blaming God for the hurt sustained. Or, it could be just plain arrogance.

(3) The final step is to accept the gift of faith that God wants to bestow on those who are willing to receive it and then ask the Lord for it.

If Bill's doubts seem to stem primarily from depression, anxiety and deep-seated emotional problems, it might be advisable to refer him for pastoral counseling, as this may be beyond your competence to handle.

Dryness

Difficulties presented: Evelyn comes to you expressing the feeling that God doesn't seem to be near, and that prayer is meaningless and useless. She's tried a lot of different types of prayer that have been recommended to her, like centering prayer, charismatic prayer, scripture reflections, and attending daily mass when she can. No matter what she does, she doesn't feel like the Lord is listening, but rather is unappreciative of her efforts. Evelyn is in mid-life and is quite discouraged, yet doesn't want to give up the life of prayer. But how to go on? What would you recommend?

Underlying meaning: Often a person who is in mid-life feels that she doesn't know how to go forward in prayer. Frequently, pressing duties will make finding time for prayer difficult, if not next to impossible. Thus, prayer seems to dry up and God and the things of God seem unreal compared to the activities and demands of everyday life. The challenge is to walk by faith and to trust the faith of others, of the church, and of our forebears in order to let ourselves be carried when our own faith has grown weak and dim.

Suggestions: As a director, ask Evelyn if there is any particular type of prayer that appeals to her, like aspirations, the rosary, the mass and scripture. Since Evelyn may not have much time, suggest starting again with a little bit at a time. Also suggest that Evelyn try to remember some time in the past when she felt close to God, and ask her to pray for renewal of the graces of that time, as well as for new graces to see the Lord in everyday life. Perhaps, for those who can afford it financially or timewise, a time of retreat, or special activity such as a prayer group, scripture study or centering prayer group, would be helpful.

Emotional Pain with God

Difficulties presented: Judy feels emotional pain in her relationship to God. She feels that God has been cold, aloof and sometimes strict with her in prayer and in her life. She wonders if there is some type of prayer or procedure that she can follow to receive relief from this situation. She has heard of the healing of memories as well as imagining herself on God's lap and being hugged like a child, but she is a little embarrassed to try things like that. What would you advise such a person to do?

Underlying meaning: First of all it would be good to listen to Judy, because the story of God's so-called wrong deeds need to be heard. As Judy experiences the director as a compassionate, caring person, she will probably be more willing to hear what he or she has to say in return. One of the things that we can say is that God has promised good to us. We as directors don't have all the answers as to why the person is experiencing pain with God, but we can explain that it is difficult to believe in and give in to the love of the Lord if there has been personal brokenness from early childhood experiences, spiritual abuse from religious authorities, or perhaps even a misinterpretation of what God is saying or try-ing to do in our lives.

It could be, however, that God really is being strict with Judy, as he may want to discipline her—in love—as one of his beloved children, so that she can grow in holiness (Cf. Heb 11).

Suggestions: The director would do well to encourage Judy to persevere in prayer, even if it is uncomfortable. Judy should be encouraged to express these painful feelings to the Lord and ask him to help her discern what the reason is for the letdown in prayer. It might be helpful to read books like *Disappointment with God* by Philip Yancey or *Please Let Me Know You, God* by Dr. Larry Stephens. These two books might serve a person yearning to heal his or her negative feelings toward God, a need that is often overlooked in Catholic circles. Both Judy and the director should pray for the directee to believe more deeply in and to be able to experience the love of the Father and Jesus because, no matter what the reason is for this emotional pain, God wants to minister to the person's neediness and heal all wounds, even those that he may have inflicted himself, as he promised in scripture.

Faith

Difficulties presented: Joshua feels that he is lacking in faith, even though he prays a great deal and tries to be faithful by attending mass and receiving the sacraments. It seems that when something unexpected happens in Joshua's life, it sometimes catches him off guard and he feels lost and doesn't know where God is hiding when he needs him the most. What do you ask about in this situation?

Underlying meaning: Joshua understandably wants to know why God doesn't seem to show up when he needs him the most. Of course it is not easy to tell the directee this, but the scriptures and the lives and writings of the saints are a storehouse of knowl-edge and an encouragement to persevere in seeking the Lord and to believe in the sun even when it isn't shining. It would be easy for the Lord to permit us to always have consolation and for the sun to always be shining, but we wouldn't grow in Christian virtue and persevere in the faith if it were all too easy. The writings of scripture, for instance Hebrews 11 and 12, tell us of the perseverance of the saints of the Old Testament and of the discipline of the Lord, and that Jesus is our example in suffering, death and resurrection. The writings of the saints elaborate on the same theme: namely, that alongside the light of infused contemplation there is also the dark night of the soul of St. John of the Cross. Many of us may not attain so-called mystical heights, but still will experience our own hills and valleys.

Suggestions: We should ask the Lord to help us to believe in him and trust in him no matter what experience we are having in prayer or in life in general. We should also pray for a way out, because he promised that we would not be tried beyond our strength, but that he would provide a way out (1 Cor 10:13).

Guidance

Difficulties presented: Christine wants to do God's will in big and little things but wonders whether God always wants the hardest thing, or the thing that she wants the least, precisely because it would constitute a mortification for her. Christine tends to be somewhat masochistic, especially since she has had some directors who taught her that doing God's will necessarily entails hardship, and that if it is too easy or pleasing to us, it is probably not of the Lord.

Christine has heard that God puts the desire for what he wants into our heart, so that what we most want ourselves is probably what God wants too, providing it is something good. She is a little skeptical, as she thinks that this is too easy. What is your view on this subject, and what comes to light as you attempt to work with the directee?

Underlying meaning: Christine should be commended for

wanting God's will in everything, as that is more than many people are willing to do. Some points to remember in connection with the will of God are: (1) God wants abundant life for us; God wants whatever is most life-giving for us, as well as for the other people who are in our lives. (2) Sometimes God asks us to carry a certain cross for a long time, but somehow he gives us the strength and courage to bear it if we ask him. (3) God doesn't always ask us to do the hardest thing, just because it is hard. Jesus said that he wanted to give us his joy and that he wanted our joy to be full (Jn 16:24). This is something that we sometimes tend to forget. We should be wary if someone is trying to lay a burden on us that God himself wouldn't ask us to carry. Beware if someone tries to control us and tell us that something is God's will, especially if we feel that it is not life-giving for us. This is tyranny, as Jesus came to set us free from the tyranny of the devil and of people who want to use us for their own purposes and for their own needs.

Suggestions: Explain to Christine that God wants abundant life for her in this life insofar as that is possible, and eternal life in heaven for her even more. Even though God sometimes permits suffering, he is not a sadist, like some people—even spiritual people— can be. Encourage Christine to pray to the Lord and to let his love become manifest to her and to show her how to please him in everything. Also, point out to her that God is happy with our efforts to please him, even if our response is not always perfect. We should strive to gear our knowledge of God's will according to his word, in particular as it is revealed in the gospel accounts.

Healing

Difficulties presented: Claudia, who is in spiritual direction with you, feels a need for spiritual healing. She is very wounded, both emotionally and spiritually, because of traumatic experiences early in life—as well as unhealthy relationship patterns which persisted later in life due to the early patterns learned in childhood. Claudia is open to the healing of the Lord in whatever way that he wants to touch her. She is willing to believe in God for supernatural healing, that is, healing through prayer, as well as the more conventional route of healing through psychotherapy and self-help groups (like the twelve-step groups). She also knows that God can touch her through her private prayer, although that is somewhat the problem. She finds it difficult to be open to the Lord in private prayer, because she feels so much emotional pain when she prays. As Claudia's director, what do you recommend?

Underlying meaning: In the present day there are many different groups of people who claim to be able to be the channel of healing to a person in need. Some of these people are quite sensitive and do seem to possess a genuine gift of healing. One thing that comes to mind is that Claudia should be asked where healing is desired. A healing should not be forced upon her, as if she has an obligation to accept the ministry of the person who has the gift of healing in a blind, undiscriminating way. Many have found the healing of memories to be beneficial, but sometimes those who have the gift of healing can think that they know better than the directee and even God himself. This is especially true in a case where too much advice is given, such as at times when the celibate life is discouraged in deference to marriage.

Discretion should be used in going to people with a healing ministry. Often those that make use of the sacraments—like the anointing of the sick, eucharist and reconciliation—are more helpful than those where people are just prayed over by lay people.

Often when a person receives a healing, no attempt is made to help the person integrate the healing into the fabric of everyday life. Thus the person doesn't know how to go on with life as a healed person.

Suggestions: It would be good, if Claudia decides to go to a person with a gift of healing, to make sure that he or she is a sensitive minister and, if possible, trained in psychology and certainly adhering to the general teachings and traditions of the Catholic Church. For instance, a person with the gift of healing should not try to heal a person of a spirit of celibacy, if the directee is a single person seeking a celibate life. Also, the minister should not be judgmental and try to lay a guilt trip on a person who has committed some particular sin. If necessary, the directee should be referred to the sacrament of reconciliation, but the minister should not demean the directee for whatever was done. Also, there should be no put-downs about emotional problems.

If the directee has been ministered to and has received some emotional or even physical healing, it would be advisable for the directee to continue in spiritual direction and discuss her feelings about the healing that took place in order to be able to integrate the healing into life, and to learn how to live without the problem, whatever it may have been. Keeping a journal might also be helpful, and the directee and director might pray for the Lord to protect the directee from regressing and claim the resurrection power of Jesus in the directee's life.

Locutions

Difficulties presented: Paul comes and tells you that he has been hearing from God, and that God has told him to uproot his life in Michigan and move to Ohio, as he will be able to minister better there. Paul wants to know whether the divine command should be followed or not, and if so, how should it be carried out? Paul is a young single man with many gifts. He is just getting established in his profession and is weighing the options. He wants to be open to what God wants, but believes that God also gave him common sense to use in conjunction with the locutions that he hears from the Lord. What do you think about this situation?

Underlying meaning: St. Teresa of Avila as well as St. John of the Cross give us an extended teaching on the discernment of locutions (*Life* 25, *Interior Castle* VI:3:1ff, *Ascent II*:28-30). Briefly, St. Teresa says the following: (1) Divine locutions bring peace and a desire to praise God. (2) They come true if something is predicted, even if the prediction doesn't seem likely to come about and people contradict it. (3) A person has to listen to it whether he or she wants to or not; the ear cannot be closed to it. (4) The words are clear and often unexpected, thus they are not made up by the recipient and are not the result of delusion. (5) The individual feels graced and grows in humility and the fruits of the Spirit in general, if it is of the Lord.

St. John mainly describes the dangers of locutions and tells us to disregard them as much as possible. However, he distinguishes three different categories: (1) the successive locution, (2) the formal locution, and (3) the substantial locution.

Suggestions: Explain to Paul the dangers, but also the possibilities of God speaking through a locution. Help him to realize that not every vibe or inner stirring is a divine locution, but that these experiences need to be sorted out in spiritual direction. Ask for examples of when and what the Lord seemed to speak to Paul and go through a discernment process, asking yourself whether the above criteria apply to the locution or not. If it seems to be of the Lord, tell Paul to still be careful, but to listen to the Lord and use sound judgment, that is, weigh the pros and cons of moving, and if possible, give the move a trial run. He should try to get oriented toward what the situation in the new state would be, and ask the Lord for continued guidance. He should trust that God will continue to confirm the decision by his consolation, and perhaps by ease in getting re-established in the new location. If this locution doesn't seem to meet the above criteria, advise the directee not to pay any attention to it, as it is possible that the devil or the imagination had a hand in it.

Mansions

Difficulties presented: Lois, the directee, wants to know where she is along the road of prayer. She has heard of the *Interior Castle* and wants to know what St. Teresa thinks about where she, Lois, is on the spiritual path. She realizes that knowing where we are on the spiritual path may have its advantages and disadvantages. We can get so preoccupied with evaluating our place on the spiritual path that we lose interest in loving God and neighbor. Lois asks you for advice on this subject, hoping that you can give her some perspective. How do you explain about spiritual growth and progress to her?

Underlying meaning: It might be good to have a general idea of what to expect on the road of prayer, and therefore reading St. Teresa of Avila's *Interior Castle* is a smart thing to do in order to have a general orientation of what can happen in the life of prayer. However, to think that God is going to bring about, for all who pray, exactly what he did for St. Teresa, is asking for disappointment and disillusionment. St. Teresa herself says that even if we have advanced in the practice of prayer, it is sometimes still necessary to go back to the beginning and reflect on the basic facts of our faith: the life, death, and resurrection of Jesus (*Life* 13). She believes that we should continue to practice whatever kind of prayer we can until God lifts us up into union with himself, if he is going to do that and if we are open to it.

Most prayerful people will know after awhile that God doesn't follow the same pattern all the time, but that he does new and unexpected things. But it is not true, as some people seem to believe, that God is unreliable, just because we don't know what he is going to do. God does not suddenly decide to abandon us or leave us devastated without him at the center of everything.

Suggestions: Explain to Lois, as best you can, something about the different stages of prayer, but also try to make clear that things don't always happen in that sequence, or in exactly the way St. Teresa and others describe it as happening to themselves. Each person's faith history is unique and God deals with each of us individually.

Meditation

Difficulties presented: David asks whether you can recommend some type of Christian meditation exercises. He is a beginner in prayer and wants to learn how to pray more adequately and encounter the Lord in prayer. He is willing to try different methods to see what suits him best, but doesn't want anything that is too structured. A couple of directors in his recent past have tried to teach him how to do some of the exercises of St. Ignatius, but he finds these too structured. He explains that he got more confused than ever and felt that he wasn't experiencing God enough in his prayer. He hopes that God has something for him besides working through Ignatius and his methods. He is interested in, but a little scared of, charismatic prayer. What would you recommend to him?

Underlying meaning: There are many different types of prayer that a Christian can undertake. All of them, if exercised properly, should be able to help us open up to receive God's grace in the life of prayer. Traditionally, different schools of spirituality have all had their own technique of meditation, and each is a little different. For instance, there are the exercises of St. Ignatius of Loyola, as well as some lesser known schools of prayer, such as the Carmelite school, the Sulpician method, the Franciscan school, etc.

At the present time, there is more emphasis on meditative reading of scripture, or maybe another spiritual book. Scripture especially lends itself to meditative reading—*lectio divina*—which has monastic origins, but is being successfully used by many people in other settings besides the monastery.

Then there is centering prayer, which also has ancient roots. It is still popular today, and seems to be helping a good number of people to open themselves to God's grace in prayer.

Conversational prayer, in which a person talks to God or Jesus about things that are on his or her mind: life, scripture passages, problems, or anything else that is of concern to the supplicant, also has much merit. All of these are useful in their time, but finally, if we persevere, we will become quiet and let the Lord himself speak in our hearts.

Prayer is a grace and we cannot force God to reveal himself to us, but he generally will if we open ourselves to receive his grace. He is in control of the relationship, not us.

Suggestions: The director might want to make David aware of the prayer options: meditated reading, centering prayer, conversation with God. There are many options besides Ignatian contemplation and charismatic prayer. All of these can be useful. Also recommended is the writing of a spiritual journal, which might include writing a letter to God or Jesus. Sometimes when we are all tied up in knots, this is the only way that we can pray. God honors this and all our attempts at communicating with him. One advantage to keeping a journal is that the praying person can see in retrospect how God has been present to him or her throughout the foregoing days, weeks, months and years. A pattern can be discerned, and David, or any directee, can rejoice that God truly is present in his life in an active, noticeable way.

Noticing

Difficulties presented: Melanie is asked to describe what she thinks is taking place during prayer. She is encouraged to notice what the Lord seems to be doing in prayer as well as her own responses to that working of the Lord within her. She feels, when she reflects on what she is experiencing in her prayer, that the Lord is eluding her, and that every time she tries to be close to him, he seems to withdraw. What can you as director do to help the directee in this process of becoming aware and responding to this prayer situation?

Underlying meaning: It can be quite a startling experience to notice the Lord in prayer for the first time. For so long the directee perhaps has said prayers without much awareness of the presence of the Lord. One day that changes and she finds herself experiencing a relationship with the Lord. It can be met with rejoicing, surprise, insecurity, disappointment (for now the directee realizes more than ever that she is accountable to the Lord, who really lives). Nevertheless, it is a great grace to become aware of the presence of God and to experience a relationship with the God of the universe whom we can call our Father (cf. Frs. Barry and Connolly, *The Practice of Spiritual Direction*).

Some directees are a little awkward when they try to describe their experience of speaking with the Lord. Others fall back on more traditional forms of expression, like: "He is the holy one; he is great and powerful." But if the directee is encouraged to continue to notice and to express what is going on between him or her and the Lord as it is perceived, the descriptions become more adept.

Suggestions: Encourage Melanie to keep a spiritual journal and to write in it especially when strong emotions are present in prayer. She might want to write what she perceives God to be like when she is feeling sad, joyful, angry, anxious, etc., in prayer. At this time, she could also describe what it is like to feel that God is eluding her. Perhaps as she is writing, she will get an idea of why God seems to be hiding from her, and what she could do in response. It could be that Melanie doesn't want the Lord to be in charge of the relationship, but that she wants to be in control. As Melanie gets in touch with her own emotions and asks the Lord if he is trying to tell her something about their relationship, it will gradually become apparent what the Lord is trying to convey—his love and concern, a teaching, correction, etc. The journal will aid Melanie in remembering the feelings and her responses at prayer and thus to get in touch with the dynamics between her and her Lord.

Overly Active

Difficulties presented: Keith wants to live for the Lord, but mainly through other people. He feels like it is a waste of time to pray, because nothing happens when he prays anyway and action is needed in order to help others. Often he feels that some of his fellow Christians are hypocrites, because he feels they are overly pious—always praying, but not doing anything. He feels that maybe he ought to pray because it is the right thing to do, but he doesn't want to fall into hypocrisy like so many other people who call themselves Christians. Besides, don't we have to do things ourselves, since God works through us? What advice would you give Keith?

Underlying meaning: A person who thinks that prayer is a waste of time and wants to live a purely humanitarian life is not reading the mind of Jesus or following his example and his Spirit. Jesus himself, as busy as he was with ministering to people, always found time to pray. In fact, he would at times escape the crowds of people with their pressing needs, just to commune with his Father. If we think that we are more indispensable than Jesus in meeting other people's needs, we are kidding ourselves. Jesus went to pray to remain centered on his Father and his Father's love and will. That way he could remain true to his mission of bringing God's kingdom among the people, instead of being a self-appointed do-gooder without the power of the Spirit.

Suggestions: If Keith is open to it, ask him to read and reflect—if need be with a journal—on some of the passages in scripture where Jesus prays in solitude (Mk 1:35), as well as in public. Think of the sacerdotal prayer for the disciples and all those who would come to believe in him. Think of Jesus's prayer before the raising of Lazarus (Jn 11), of Jesus' prayer on the cross (Mt 27:26; Lk 23:34; Jn 19:25-30). Jesus prayed everywhere and anywhere, so shouldn't we do the same? If Keith cannot see this reality about Jesus and the life of prayer, perhaps he could benefit from psychological counseling. He might have a problem with being needed too much—with being indispensable. Perhaps a deep feeling of personal inadequacy is at the root of being overly busy at the expense of prayer. If feasible, point out that possibility to Keith, and see if he would be open to therapy.

Overly Intellectual

Difficulties presented: Jack enjoys his theological studies as well as other intellectual pursuits, and perhaps would like to teach theology at a university. However, he doesn't think much of the practice of prayer because he thinks it is too subjective and that feelings get in the way of intellectual honesty. But a good friend advised Jack to look you up, as he felt Jack had something to gain from spirituality. Jack came to you because he wanted to placate his friend. How would you respond to this challenge?

Underlying meaning: Our intellect and intellectual activities have been given to us by the Lord and he wants us to use them to glorify him. Faith and reason should not be opposed if they are used properly. Sometimes intellectually-gifted people have been exposed to the wrong type of spirituality—perhaps a legalistic or saccharine spirituality that is inappropriate for them and doesn't take into account the personal needs of a person such as Jack. There are many devout intellectuals in the history of Christianity to take as an example: Thomas Aquinas, Duns Scotus, Augustine, John Henry Newman, not to mention St. Paul himself. Clearly, spirituality isn't just for the ignorant. However, Jack will not make much progress if he comes just to please someone else. He needs to have his own motivation in order to be open to the Lord.

Suggestions: Explain to Jack, the reluctant directee that he has to want direction himself in order to benefit from it. If he is open to it, perhaps you could suggest that he read some of Paul's letters, as well as a commentary on his spiritual doctrine contained in the letter— for instance, a study of his teaching on the Holy Spirit or the spiritual gifts. Another suggestion is for Jack to read some of the passages on spiritual matters from St. Thomas Aquinas, as he too writes on prayer and the spiritual gifts. This might help a gifted person like

Jack to realize that spirituality is not just for the weak or intellectually dull. And if Jack also needs to read on faith and reason, there are many books available on the subject from a Christian point of view. Just getting to know in general what the Christian faith and spirituality are all about can be pursued by deeper studies of classical as well as contemporary masters of the spiritual life, plus some church and Christian intellectual history.

An intellectually-oriented person should not be told to put the mind aside and just to have faith. It doesn't work like that for most. Rather, the mind needs to be put to work in the process of discovering the fullness of the faith.

Overly Spiritual

Difficulties presented: Colleen wants to be totally detached so as to be closer to God. She feels that contact with people often makes her feel less close to God, because she can't keep her mind on the spiritual presence of God as she wishes. She therefore wants to limit contact with other people, as she feels this would enhance her life of prayer and help her to experience God more directly. Alone she feels more single-minded. What might you consider when discussing this with Colleen?

Underlying meaning: Other people are not supposed to be considered as a distraction from our life of prayer and communion with God. We Christians believe that God himself became man, that is, became a human being like us. So it must not be wrong to be a human being or to find God through other people. It is true that people can distract us from prayer, but so can a lot of other things, such as all kinds of sin—perhaps in this case spiritual pride, including fear of deeper relationships with people. St. John says that if we don't love our brother or sister whom we can see, we cannot love the God we cannot see (1 Jn 4:20-21). Certainly there are those who are called to a monastic vocation, but these are the exception. And probably these people would tell us that they are praying for other people and living elbow to elbow with others in the monastery. So monasticism and prayer aren't an escape from other people.

Suggestions: Point out to someone like Colleen, who feels that other people are keeping her from prayer, it is good to have some solitude for explicit attention to God and the things of God, but that this solitude is to be balanced with being with and giving loving service to our neighbor.

Pettiness in Doing God's Will

Difficulties presented: Kevin wants to do God's will in everything to the point of trying to discern relatively unimportant things like whether to call his mother, open the mail, or go to the store. He feels that in the past he often has not heeded the Lord's call and has been disobedient to God in his daily life. He has heard that he should do the will of God in everything, not just some things. He is afraid of offending the Lord by not listening, so he tries to listen for guidance in every little detail. In so doing, he wastes a lot of time that could be used for productive work for the kingdom. What would you do to counsel an overly conscientious directee like this?

Underlying meaning: A person like Kevin can be obsessive-compulsive about doing God's will, just as he is about anything else. If a person is too strict about trying to discern every little detail concerning doing God's will, such as whether or not to wash the car, it can become a bondage instead of a freeing experience, like our Father in heaven intended. Just as in everything else, too much is not healthy.

However, the scriptures show us that God does want to be involved in everything in our lives as much as possible, and sometimes he will give indications about his will in smaller things; but he doesn't bind us with anxiety. If he doesn't give us any insights, we should not pray for hours over each little decision. It could be that if we are in bondage to anxiety about God's will, we have been listening unintentionally to the evil spirit, who wants us to be tied up in knots. We can be freed from this by learning from helpful Christian books about the freedom of true discernment of God's will and by praying for the Lord's freedom in our hearts.

One good thing that the overly anxious discerner has rightly understood is that God wants to be a part of everything we do. Thus discernment is a way of life and not just a procedure to be followed for the big decisions of life, such as what vocation to choose—especially the discernment of a religious, celibate vocation. Rather, discernment is meant, for the people of God, to be a way of walking daily with the Lord and seeking after his will for their daily lives.

Suggestions: An overly anxious person needs to be reminded that seeking the will of God in all things is good, but that like anything else it can be perverted if carried to extremes. It doesn't seem reasonable that God wants us to be impaired in our daily activities by praying twenty minutes about whether to take a walk, or watch TV first. This is defeating the purpose of a loving awareness of the Father's care for all the details of our lives.

Kevin should be told that God certainly will respect our own judgment in most of these small decisions and that we can still keep him in the center of our lives by praying with aspirations. If he has something to say about what we are doing or planning to do, he usually will make it clear to us by a locution or by giving us a certain idea or feeling. It takes experience in the spiritual life to discern some of these things with any regular success, if we want to call it that. However, we can ask the Lord to make himself known and he probably will in one way or another (cf. Graham Fitzpatrick, *How to Recognize God's Voice*).

If this anxiety about discerning and doing God's will proves to be a deeply-rooted problem that isn't alleviated after some instruction like the above, it might be good to gently suggest that the person see a psychotherapist and/or psychiatrist for proper therapy and/or medication. There is some quite helpful medication for obsessive-compulsive persons, although there are some side effects. Nevertheless, it may be worth looking into, if the situation warrants it.

Practicing the Presence of God

Difficulties presented: Barbara explains that she tries to think about the presence of God during the day, but feels that she is not always successful. She has been trying to have a regular prayer period for some time, but finds it more difficult to keep Jesus in her mind while going about her business. The affairs of the day tend to distract her in such a way that she finds it difficult to return and center on the Lord. She is not used to the discipline, as it requires a certain kind of sacrifice: giving up time normally spent in daydreaming to concentrate on the Lord. This means letting the Lord into every aspect of daily life and not trying to confine him to scheduled prayer time. She prays for help and sometimes at the most unexpected times the Lord makes his presence felt. Barbara wonders how to acknowledge the Lord, as she is afraid that people will think she is strange if they see her praying in the midst of her activities. How would you respond to this?

Underlying meaning: The practice of the presence of God has been discussed in the book (by that name) written by Brother Lawrence, and I refer you to that. However, it is common knowledge among those familiar with the life of prayer, that the felt presence of God comes and goes as the Lord desires and we are able to receive it and be open to it. St. Teresa of Avila says that she sometimes felt the presence of the Lord in prayer (chapter ten of her *Life*) but also almost anytime that she was a little bit recollected.

Perhaps Barbara didn't know how to be recollected and thus was missing the visitations of God. As she prays for awareness of the presence of God, this awareness will be given as a gift.

Suggestions: Sometimes we really cannot stop what we are doing and we just have to let go of attending to the presence of the Lord. We can trust that the Lord will visit us again when we are more able to be consciously present to him. At other times, however, although we can stop, we feel embarrassed to do so because we are afraid that people around us will notice us praying in the middle of everything for no apparent good reason.

I struggled with that for years on my jobs and sometimes fled to the bathroom to pray in a stall where nobody could see me except the good Lord. I know from talking to others that they sometimes do or have done similar things in order to have some privacy with the Lord during the day.

There are also techniques, like that of centering prayer, which are available to gain some discipline in daily prayer. As a person devotes some explicit time to prayer each day, it will become easier to notice and accept visitations from the Lord throughout the day. Some people keep a pebble in their pocket, and remember to turn toward the Lord when they feel the pebble.

Prayer Difficulties

Difficulties presented: Jody is beginning to seek deeper prayer and wonders if you can give some suggestions for getting deeper into the life of the Spirit. She used to be Lutheran, but now is Catholic. She likes the Catholic tradition of spirituality, although she confesses not to know much about it; that is, she feels she still has much to learn about the Catholic spiritual tradition. She has been reading her Bible for many years, ever since she was young, but feels that the Bible, as such, doesn't really give concrete instructions on how to pray. She wants some pointers on how to pray. She does not seem to be inclined toward charismatic prayer as the emotionalism tends to turn her off, but likes to focus on Jesus and God the Father. What could you suggest to her in the way of prayer?

Underlying meaning: There are as many ways to pray as there are people, and Jody should do whatever works for her. However, there are certain types of prayer that have been recommended throughout the centuries in the history of Christianity. One of them is meditating on scripture, that is, doing meditative reading on one of the psalms, or perhaps a passage about Jesus performing a cure, or the resurrection narratives, etc.

It seems to me that in the past many devout people have put too much emphasis on meditation on the passion at the expense of the resurrection. St. Teresa of Avila liked to reflect on the passion of Christ, and this certainly has a place. She was also fond of reflecting on the resurrection of Jesus, depending on her mood and how the Spirit led her (*Way of Perfection* 26). St. Teresa also enjoyed just imagining Jesus at her side and talking to him from her heart as an intimate friend, indeed as her divine Spouse.

Suggestions: Recommend to Jody that she continue to use the gospel accounts for prayer, as they show us most of all who Jesus is and what his message is to us. Jesus also tells us that whoever has seen him has seen the Father (Jn 14:9), so he also shows us what God is like. Encourage Jody to ask for the grace of friendship with Jesus and then accept it in faith, knowing that it is being granted. Also remind Jody to persevere in dry times and in times of boredom with prayer, meditation and the like.

If Jody still wants to learn more about the Catholic tradition of prayer, recommend a shared prayer group, as well as reading about the spiritual teachings of St. Teresa of Avila. There are many good and helpful books available about St. Teresa and her prayer experience, as well as innumerable other works on this topic. Recommended are works by Thomas Green, and by Thomas Dubay, as well as Benedict Groeschel.

Prayer of Quiet

Difficulties presented: Sue is apparently advancing in prayer. She is beginning to experience the prayer of quiet. This can be deduced from the phenomena that she describes: a sweetness in the experience of the Lord's presence, a desire to sit and be with the Lord for an hour at a time without having to resort to prayer books or *lectio divina,* a slight deepening and increasing of the rhythm of breathing. These are the telltale signs of the prayer of quiet. What can Sue do to cooperate with God's action in this situation?

Underlying meaning: The prayer of quiet is the beginning of the mystical grades of prayer as described by St. Teresa of Avila in her *Interior Castle* (Mansion 4) as well as her *Life.* This favor, although exalted, is still a fairly common occurrence for those who have tried to persevere on the pathway of prayer.

Some of the characteristics of this stage of mystical prayer are: (1) great liberty of spirit (2) filial fear of God and great care not to offend him (3) profound confidence in God (4) love of mortification and suffering (5) deep humility (6) disdain for worldly pleasures, and (7) growth in all the virtues.

Suggestions: According to Fr. Jordan Aumann, the following guidelines should be followed:

1. Never attempt to force the prayer of quiet to happen.
2. Cooperate with the movement of the Spirit as soon as it is perceived.
3. Do not disturb the quiet of the will by being anxious about and trying to attend to distractions.
4. Scrupulously avoid any occasion of offending God.
5. Never give up praying no matter how difficult it may seem at times. For more information on what to do in the prayer of quiet, I refer you to page 339 of *Spiritual Theology* by Fr. Jordan Aumann.

Presence of God

Difficulties presented: Terry reports sometimes sensing the presence of God, at times outside of prayer and at other times during the explicit time set aside for prayer each day. However, Terry is finding that he cannot control—that is, turn the experience on or off—at will, although sometimes if he asks the Lord to "stay awhile," the Lord seems to give in and lets Terry "have him" so to speak. Terry finds this disconcerting and sometimes even frustrating. How can you help him adjust to this experience of the coming and going of the sense of the presence of the Lord?

Underlying meaning: We as Christians believe that God is sovereign, that we can't control what he does in his relationship to us. Nevertheless, he has given us a covenant in the blood of Jesus. God gave his only begotten son, so that no matter how it feels, we have the assurance of his love and faithfulness. Sometimes it may be that he wants to test our faith and see if we'll be loyal to him, who gave his all for us, or he may want to help us realize that we are dependent on his mercy and that he is in control of the relationship, not us. The Lord truly gives himself to those who give themselves to him. Sometimes we get attached to consolation instead of to the Lord himself. This is like a spiritual codependency, being dependent on the feeling, instead of on the lover himself.

Nevertheless, it sometimes seems that the Lord indulges himself in our desire for his felt presence, simply because we are his beloved children and he sometimes wants to show that he is a doting father in heaven, who loves to give his children sweets from time to time (*The Ascent of Mount Carmel* II:21:3). But as St. John of the Cross says, he then puts us down so that we can walk on our own two feet (*Dark Night of the Soul* I:1:2), but with him ever near, even if his presence is not felt.

Suggestions: Terry can be encouraged to tell the Lord how it feels that he comes and goes; when he leaves, so to speak, it seems that he is abandoning him. Terry can be advised to ask the Lord to heal the fear of abandonment, and to reflect on the scripture passages that speak of the Lord's tender, never-failing love, such as Isaiah 49, where the Lord consoles us, saying that even if a mother could forget her infant, still he will never forget us. Or Isaiah 54, where the Lord says that he will honor his everlasting covenant with us, even though he hid his face awhile in anger. He promises that his tender love will win out and that he will heal all of our wounds, even the ones that he inflicted on us himself when he disciplined us.

Presence of God

Difficulties presented: Bernie is desirous of having more awareness of the presence of God during the day. He frequently goes to mass on the weekdays and says morning and bedtime prayers, but often forgets that God is always present. He feels that he has too many distractions in his daily life, and that he could increase in self-discipline. Bernie asks what can be done, as he wants to live with God during the day in a conscious way.

Underlying meaning: The Bible admonishes us to pray always. Of course, that is not feasible for most of us in the literal sense. As a matter of fact, even monks and hermits have to eat, sleep and work sometimes, and thus cannot pray continually, at least in an explicit way. So we shouldn't be discouraged if it is sometimes difficult to be aware of the Lord during the day and to focus on his presence in a world that does not remind us continually of the Lord's presence as the monastic environment does. This doesn't mean that we shouldn't try, however. The saints and all people who have striven for holiness throughout the ages have tried to retain some awareness of the presence of God in the midst of everyday tasks.

Suggestions: Some people say short prayers throughout the day as an attempt to have conscious contact with God on an ongoing basis. Some may take a coffee break or lunch break with the Lord and try to read a couple of lines of scripture. Homemakers might want to try praying the rosary during the day while the children are at school or taking a nap. Business people may try to attend mass on their lunch hour if there is an opportunity to do so, such as in downtown Chicago at St. Peter's Church where there are eleven masses every working day, four of which are during the lunch hour. There are many ways of remembering the presence of God if we really want to. Develop your own method of giving the Lord some attention during the day and then stick to it!

Presence of God

Difficulties presented: Carlotta often experiences the presence of God—if it is the presence of God—in an uncomfortable way during prayer and off and on during the day. Carlotta has tried different things in prayer: spiritual reading, being quiet, asking the Lord if there is something he wants her to know. But it all seems in vain. She feels very anxious and wonders what the reason is for this unsettled feeling. She asks herself whether God is trying to convey some message to her or whether something is the matter. What would you tell Carlotta?

Underlying meaning: In his book, *How to Recognize God's Voice,* Graham Fitzpatrick explains that sometimes God will communicate with us by giving us an uneasy feeling, if we are considering something that is against his commandments and will. If we are getting this uneasy, queasy feeling in the stomach, it would be good to consider if there is something that we are doing against God and his ways. However, this is not always the cause of discomfort during prayer. It can be neurotic anxiety that needs to be healed by the Lord, or may even stem from an attack by the devil, the adversary of the human race, who wants us to keep away from prayer.

Although it is not a popular notion in the present age to believe in the devil, it is sometimes good to remember that scripture speaks of the evil one. Many Christians, as well as some people of other religions, have had experience of evil spirits. The scriptures tell us to be armed with the helmet of faith (see Ephesians 6).

Suggestions: Make Carlotta aware of the above considerations. Pray with her for guidance, asking the Lord to make it clear what the reason is for this discomfort during prayer. Perhaps it is a combination of things, as is often the case in human life. Just explaining the possible causes of anxiety and uncomfortable feelings in prayer can sometimes make the directee aware of where the cause could lie. An examination of conscience is a gentle way of becoming aware of what is needed. Also, prayer for healing of emotional pain that sometimes surfaces during meditation could be helpful. If the anxiety persists, professional help may be indicated.

Presence of God

Difficulties presented: Margaret often experiences the warm, soothing presence of God during prayer and feels that prayer gives hope, strength and courage. However, Margaret wants to hold on to these experiences and wonders what can be done. She is afraid that when God seems to withhold consolations, he is angry with her and doesn't love her anymore. What would you advise Margaret about holding on to consolations?

Underlying meaning: It is sometimes said that our God is the God of all consolations, but the God of consolations is not the same as the consolations of God. In the first case, we allow the Lord, or rather the experience, to come and go, believing that God himself remains the same all through the alternation of experiences. The danger of hanging onto consolation is not loving God for himself, and/or developing a kind of unhealthy dependence on the consolations of God. We feel that we have to have them, or life can't go on. They may also be seen as a mark of God's approval of us, and we may feel that if we don't experience consolation that something is the matter—that God is mad at us or doesn't love us any more.

Suggestions: In order to avoid this kind of trap of codependency, it is good to be saturated with the teaching of the scriptures on what God is like. Then, if we don't experience consolations whenever we want them, we won't be devastated, because we'll know that God is our friend, lover and father, even if we feel absolutely nothing—that is, even if our heart seems ice cold and we experience no consolation at all. Also, if we know and believe what the scriptures say, we can reject religious experiences that don't reveal God as loving and caring for us. For instance, if we feel that something we think is spiritual says that it hates us and wants to harm us, we can be sure that it is not the Lord, and we can reject it and command it to leave in the name of Jesus.

Prophecy

Difficulties presented: A young woman named Monica comes to you for guidance. Some people in her prayer group who have the gift of prophecy have been proclaiming to her that it is God's will for her to get married to a particular young man who is also in the prayer group. She likes the young man but doesn't want to marry him because of an age difference, because she wants her freedom before she commits herself to marriage, and also because she wants it to be her decision and not theirs. He doesn't feel that he's ready for marriage but he doesn't want to be disobedient to the Lord's call upon his life. She too is willing to do what God wants, but wonders whether the prophecy given was an authentic prophecy or whether it was just made up. They are both very embarrassed and confused. What do you think they should do about this situation?

Underlying meaning: Of course it is important to do God's will, but who says that someone else can discern what God's will is for a person's life? This couple has to discern with prayer before the Lord, look at the circumstances and ask themselves questions such as: are we suitable for each other, do we love each other, are we ready for marriage, do we want to get married at all?

Another person can serve as a co-discerner in humility to the persons who have to make a decision, but they cannot pretend to make the decision for the people who have to carry it out.

Suggestions: As a spiritual director, it would be advisable to make the young persons aware of their dignity and need for as much freedom as possible in Christ. Let them know that others should not be allowed to manipulate them through prophecies or other means. It should be clear from the standpoint of church teaching on human dignity that there is no moral obligation to follow prophecies, especially if they are in opposition to one's own conscience and prayerful discernment.

Religious Addiction

Difficulties presented: Ken goes to church several times a day, and yet feels it isn't enough. He wonders if he has really worshipped God worthily or whether he should try to do more. In the meantime family and job are being neglected and the boss is about ready to fire him for tardiness and poor attendance at work. How would you advise Ken in his situation?

Underlying meaning: There actually is such a thing as religious addiction. As good as it is to practice our faith and give honor to God, the Bible tells us that we have to work for a living as far as we are able. Thus, unless we are sick or disabled, or unless we have a religious vocation for a monastic community, or have enough money so that we don't have to work, we have a serious obligation to provide for ourselves and our families by working on a regular basis. Even monks have work time scheduled in their day, to help support and maintain their monasteries.

Suggestions: You might have to point out to Ken that religious observance can be carried to an extreme. There is such a thing as a wrong use of religion and Ken should be made aware of the fact that this really can happen. Perhaps it might be beneficial to suggest that the directee attend a twelve-step group. Although most of them were originally meant to deal with alcohol or drug abuse, there are now groups such as Codependents Anonymous, Emotions Anonymous and other such organizations that can help to deal with religious addiction as well.

Many people have found benefit from them, and the directee can talk about almost anything that is on his mind at these meetings. Also, Ken should be admonished to work and provide for his family and be reminded that it does not give a good witness to the Lord to be negligent on the job.

Religious Vocation

Difficulties presented: Joyce, a middle-aged, single, career woman, was told at a retreat after a certain religious experience that she might have a religious vocation, that is, a vocation to the celibate life in a convent. She is interested and applies at a couple of places. She prays about it and feels some attraction. However, she has difficulty maintaining a regular prayer life and often skips her prayers when some other attractive activity comes along, such as going to the movies, watching television, or talking on the phone. Joyce also often prefers to sleep in instead of getting up to go to mass in the morning. However, she goes to church faithfully on Sundays, tries to pray when she feels like it and attempts to be a good person. How would you counsel Joyce if she came to you for advice?

Underlying meaning: It seems that Joyce believes that a religious vocation will just sort of "happen," and that somehow at some future date it will all come together. However, she feel little or no desire to seek God in the ordinary ways that a person who wishes to give herself to him in the celibate life usually would.

It seems that she is hanging onto her desire for a religious vocation because she perceives it as a higher vocation than single life or marriage, and she wants to think of herself as being special to the Lord and to other people. However, the union with God, the communal living, and the life of service(sometimes doing things that aren't pleasing and giving up attachment to one's family) are not always attractive. Thus Joyce is not really attracted to what makes up a religious vocation, only the *idea* of being a religious.

Suggestions: Suggest to Joyce that she try a weekend or a couple of weeks of living in a convent and see if it still appeals to her. Perhaps she will realize it is not all she thought it was and that it is not for her. If she still persists in this desire to be a religious without trying to get closer to the Lord, perhaps she needs professional counseling to help sort out her feelings. Perhaps she may realize in time that it is not for her—but until then, we may have to leave her with her illusion and assume that it meets some deep psychological need.

Remembering

Difficulties presented: As a means to getting in touch with what God or Jesus has done in Dick's personal life (that is, the life of prayer as well as the day-to-day exterior life), the director asks him to try to write a story in his spiritual journal, describing what his life with God in the past looks like from today's perspective, and what the Lord is trying now to convey to him through these actions in his life. How can you as director assist Dick in interpreting this personal history with the Lord and his special love for him?

Underlying meaning: Most of us can remember some religious experiences that we have had: high points with the Lord, when we have noticed his presence in a particular way in our lives. Those of us who have tried to cultivate the live of prayer, and perhaps have even kept a journal about what we experienced with the Lord, will be more likely to see a pattern of God's interaction with us, of his loving care and of the things that he has taught us throughout the years.

Suggestions: The director might ask Dick to write a couple of paragraphs in his journal describing one or even several times in his life when the presence of the Lord was felt in a strong and explicit way. These are milestones: they stand out from the rest of everyday life. Ask Dick to begin with the earliest one he can remember and then proceed to the present. Some people probably haven't reflected on their faith history much and will need some encouragement to think about this. Others who have tried to practice prayer on a regular basis will probably be able to put together a whole story of how God has acted and interacted with them in life, and how he has shown his special love for them as individuals.

Repressed Material

Difficulties presented: Debbie is getting into a deeper prayer life and is finding that some old—mainly painful—feelings about things that happened years ago are emerging. Debbie is bewildered, as she thought that those things had already been dealt with and were dead and buried. Also, she sometimes has unusual and bizarre dreams as well as strange daydreams or daytime experiences that are confusing. This seems to have happened mainly since the path of more systematic prayer has been followed. She wonders what God is doing to her and whether these experiences really are from the Lord. What can you do to help her?

Underlying meaning: Many people will find that a lot of painful old feelings, resentments and grudges come to the surface when they start praying in a deeper way. It is because through this deeper prayer the deeper levels of the psyche are opened up. Indeed this can sometimes be bewildering. All kinds of bizarre things can present themselves to our awareness.

It has often been observed that God allows this so that the deeper layers of our psyche can be healed. Yet sometimes we need to become aware of this repressed material in order to allow the Lord to touch and heal it, as he always wants to do. This experience can also engender guilt feelings in some of us, because we perhaps thought that we hadn't retained any grudges or other so-called negative emotions. We need to accept these feelings as normal human feelings if we have been hurt. Feelings are neither good nor bad. They just are. It is what we do with these feelings that determines whether we are acting ethically or not.

Suggestions: First of all, don't panic! Don't think that Debbie or you yourself are crazy if these strange experiences appear on the horizon. Quietly, in prayer, ask Jesus to be Lord of your unconscious and to heal any and all painful memories. It may take a while to receive a complete healing. It may be weeks, months or years. Yet if we persevere with the Lord in this healing process, we will make progress and gradually become freer and happier people.

If deeper prayer is too stressful and anxiety-provoking, try scripture meditation or some vocal prayers. A suggestion might be reading the scriptures where Jesus heals the paralytic (Mk 2), the mother-in-law of Peter (Mk 1), the woman with the blood flow (Mk 5), and raises the daughter of Jairus (Mk 5), etc. Mark's gospel is a good place to start, as the compassion and power of Jesus are especially evident in these passages.

Also, it is good to try to forgive those who have hurt us, and to receive the sacrament of reconciliation, as well as the other sacraments such as the anointing of the sick and the eucharist, in order to be healed of painful memories, grudges and resentments. Try to find a prayer partner if you can, and pray on a regular basis for the healing of each other. Also, if you find that forgiveness is a struggle, don't be discouraged. It is probably only God that can really forgive carte blanche. We weak people sometimes take a while to get over hurts, especially if they are deep. We need to realize that we can't forgive on our own strength, but need to ask the Lord to help us forgive. We also need to realize that we are loved by God as individuals, and that whatever the person who hurt us did to us does not reflect on our true worth as a human being. As we grow into wholeness, we will be more able to forgive.

Sexual Spirituality

Difficulties presented: Sharon has literally fallen in love with the Lord, but is troubled by the sexual feelings that seem to accompany prayer. She tries not to indulge herself, that is, give in to the sexual feelings, but to keep them moving, and returns to her prayer, focusing on Jesus. However, because these thoughts come to her mind, she wonders whether she is abnormal or whether she committed a serious sin. How would you advise Sharon in her perplexity?

Underlying meaning: Since we are a unity of body and spirit, it is natural for some of the communications in the spiritual life to overflow into the body. Even St. Teresa and St. John of the Cross talk about this in their writings and don't seem to be too perturbed about it. It probably wouldn't be good to try to indulge ourselves in thoughts directed toward eroticism with Jesus and/or Mary, but the fact that the feelings are present doesn't mean that we are sinning. It is what we do with the feelings that matters. Especially if the directee is younger, say a woman in her twenties or thirties, the biological clock can be giving her a hard time. The body may be overreacting to intense spiritual activity.

Suggestions: A spiritual director once said, "Try not to give it too much energy." Don't be overly preoccupied with these experiences, but try to calmly continue prayer. Just tell the Lord that you love him and accept his love and want to please him in everything. Ask him to take care of these feelings like everything else." (cf. Gerald May's *Will and Spirit,* pp.150-51).

Sloth in Prayer

Difficulties presented: A religious woman named Diane comes for consultation. She isn't getting much out of prayer, and feels that maybe she has lost her first love for Jesus, her Divine Bridegroom. She wonders whether she is losing her vocation or whether she had one in the first place.

She is feeling ministry burnout and really would like to quit sometimes, but feels that the people need her. She is caught between feeling both that she is trapped, and that she wants to persevere in the religious life because that is all she really knows, and because she made her commitment to the Lord. Something in her wants to give it another try, but she doesn't want to be a hypocrite. Diane doesn't really think that she wants to get married, but she wonders what God's true will is for her life, considering the struggles she is experiencing at the present time. How would you try to help her?

Underlying meaning: These things will take some time, honesty and prayer as well as perhaps some spiritual direction and/or counseling to sort out. Of course she can give up being a religious, but probably that would not be the first thing to consider, unless there is a good reason for it. First of all, it is recommended that she do everything she can to save her vocation, as it is a precious thing.

Suggestions: Recommended activities would be trying different types of prayer until something is found that works. She should remember to get adequate rest, as sometimes prayer seems flat when a person is fatigued. Also, learning to set limits on what other people can do in one's life and on how much responsibility can be taken on are important. However, this is sometimes easier said than done.

If all of this is tried for some time and doesn't work, then perhaps taking a leave of absence from religious life in order to pray and discern from a more removed spot might be recommended. Depending on what the outcome is of this discernment process, which might take some time, the decision should be made.

Spiritual Abuse

Difficulties presented: Donna tells a sad tale of having been given a prophecy that exhorted her to give up being overly spiritual and to try to get married. The people who gave the prophecy were going to try to find someone suitable for her to marry in order to fulfill the prophecy. Donna wanted to be and still wants to be a celibate, and asks what she should do. Donna is afraid of the wrath of God, and that he will consume her in his anger if she doesn't obey the prophecy. More than anything, however, she is afraid of losing her friends, as being in the group with them has meant a lot to her and she doesn't want to give them up.

However, it looks as though they are going to try to pressure her to comply with what was prophesied. To add to her mixed feelings, she finds it almost impossible to see herself being close to Jesus, as she has been most of her life up to now, if she were married. She wonders how a God who wants us to be close to him could ask her to embrace a lifestyle which would make that very difficult for her, if not next to impossible. How would you try to assuage her fears and give her healthy guidance?

Underlying meaning: Spiritual abuse is more common than we think. It consists in trying to lord it over someone else's faith and to try to get somebody to do what you want by manipulating the word of God and, if need be, the discernment process to serve your preconceived purposes.

Needless to say, this is a grave matter, and this is probably the kind of thing for which Jesus recommended a millstone around the neck (Mt 18:6), that is, for taking advantage of those who have been entrusted to our spiritual care and/or who are dependent on us in some way or another in the spiritual realm.

Suggestions: If you get someone like Donna as a directee, emphasize that she as an individual has to do what is right in her own heart before God about a matter like this, and if need be, with some help from an enlightened director who has the directee's temporal and eternal well-being at heart. The aim of the director should be to increase, not decrease, the amount of personal and moral freedom of the directee, and thus enable Donna, in this case, to make as free a choice as possible—free from inordinate attachments, fear, etc.

It might also be good to advise Donna to distance herself from people who try to command what she should do with her life, and who try to instill fear in her of being disobedient to a prophecy such as this one.

Spiritual Isolation

Difficulties presented: Tom is a fervent Catholic Christian who goes to daily mass, frequents the sacraments, tries to live the gospel in daily life and cultivates a regular prayer life. Tom is distressed, however, that so many of his old chums don't want much to do with him anymore. Some of his Catholic friends no longer seem to have time for him or to be interested in developing a spiritual, or any kind, of friendship with him. Tom wonders why God is permitting this trial in his life. He reasons that God is supposed to be the source of all life, but that this increase in spiritual fervor in his life has not brought more happiness, but pain, loneliness, fear and sadness. He wonders what to do to find suitable friends with whom to share his new life. Where should Tom look for spiritual friends, and how would you encourage him?

Underlying meaning: The Christian life without companions can be quite lonely, especially since there are some whom we will encounter along the way that are not in favor of our Christianity and will try to dissuade us from following the Lord. Especially in the present time,when following Christ is more of an individual decision and not a culturally supported value, it is important to try to find some like-minded wayfarers.

Suggestions: The Christian can find spiritual friends through involvement in a local parish, especially an active one, volunteering to do things there, such as lectoring, helping with special projects, etc. Also useful is trying to find a prayer group, Bible study, a men's sharing group, Cursillo group or even a Christian twelve-step group. Most of all, it is important to pray for spiritual companionship. From experience, it is a prayer that the Lord is usually eager to answer, unless he has some higher purpose (i.e., purifying loneliness) in mind.

Suicide

Difficulties presented: Steve is thinking about committing suicide in order to be with his deceased wife. He tells you that God would understand because he wants everybody to be happy and he, the mourner, would be infinitely happy to be reunited with the loved one. He is very depressed and lonely without his deceased wife. Steve reasons that God is love, and so he would certainly not punish suicide if it was done for the right reasons. Steve has heard that suicide is wrong, but feels that there are certain situations where it can be justified, such as his own situation. How would you deal with this as a director?

Underlying meaning: It is easy to think that there is nothing wrong with suicide, as well as a number of other different actions, if we are experiencing grief and other strong emotions. Such thoughts can tend to cloud our thinking. Suicide has always been considered to be a serious matter for Christians. We have only one life, and if we kill ourselves, we can't come back and do it over. While we should be merciful in our judgement of another person who has already committed suicide, God's mercy is not something that we can presume for ourselves. That is to say, just because we hope that God will be merciful to someone else who has committed suicide doesn't mean that we should try it ourselves, because God is the Lord of life and he decides when we live and when we die. We might be sorry for presuming falsely on the mercy of God, and we might not even get to be with our deceased loved ones.

Suggestions: Steve should be referred to professional counseling or therapy if possible, as the underlying issues are probably too difficult for you as a director to cope with successfully, unless you are a skilled therapist. It is good to trust in the Lord, but also to be prudent and not to suppose that we can (or even have to be able to) handle every situation. It is really okay to admit that there are some situations that we can't handle. If the person goes to a therapist and, if need be, gets appropriate medication for depression, it still might be okay to try to support the person in the faith and encourage him to try to find meaning in this life without the presence of the deceased loved one. He should be encouraged to try to find comfort from the Lord in his grief, and also to seek to build a network of relationships with people.

Temptations

Difficulties presented: Harry feels tempted with hateful and blasphemous thoughts and with ill will toward other people. He has prayed for help in overcoming these things and finds that the more he concentrates on these thoughts in an effort to rid himself of them, the worse they become. He feels that God doesn't love him because he has evil thoughts and that the Lord has not heard him in his anguished prayer for deliverance from these harassing mental experiences. He wonders whether he is doomed to hell, or whether there is really forgiveness available for him in his situation. What to do?

Underlying meaning: St. John of the Cross explains that these types of thoughts are a common form of temptation and trial permitted by God in the devout. He distinguishes a spirit of dizziness, a spirit of fornication and a spirit of blasphemy (*Dark Night of the Soul* I:14:1ff). These types of trials can be extremely humiliating to the devout, as they seek to please God in everything and fear his displeasure.

Suggestions: The best thing to do is to try to ignore all of these things, because preoccupation with them or with efforts to get rid of them simply causes a person to be obsessed and makes them worse instead of better. We should attempt to throw ourselves into the arms of the merciful love of God, knowing that we can't get rid of these things any more than we can thoughts about pink elephants. We should keep in mind that trials like these, permitted for our good, can allow us to recognize our total dependence on the mercy and power of the Lord and to teach us to rely on him and not on our own strength.

Therapy

Difficulties presented: A middle-aged woman named Bernadette comes in, asking for advice on what to do about a therapist who is exposing some of her (the therapist's) non-Christian values in the counseling sessions. Because Bernadette likes the therapist she wants to lean on her and learn from her, but she fears that she will lose her Catholic Christian faith. She wonders whether she should continue with this therapist or try to find a Christian therapist who shares her faith and values. What would you tell Bernadette in this situation?

Underlying meaning: It is sometimes difficult to find a like-minded therapist, although it often helps to pray to find one, especially if we have some religious issues to confront in therapy. It seems that almost any therapist can be of help, provided that we are firmly rooted in our faith and know what our own values are.

Sometimes we can even be a witness to the therapist if he or she is not a Christian (or Catholic Christian).

Suggestions: It is good to listen to a therapist, but we should discern for ourselves whether the assistance offered can actually be accepted as useful in our lives. Prayer and writing in a journal probably will help us to get in touch with our own feelings about what the therapist is doing as well as put us in touch with what God might be trying to say to us about what is going on in therapy.

Sometimes it might be good to share some passages from the journal with the therapist, especially if you feel that he or she is not doing what you as a Christian would want him or her to do in a certain situation. Then the issues can be discussed with the therapist and you can pray over them some more.

If the therapist is really unable or unwilling to work with you and your Christian values, you should try to see if some more suitable therapist is available. Otherwise you would only be beating your head against the wall.

Time for God

Difficulties presented: The directee is a married woman named Jennifer who loves the Lord and enjoys his company in prayer. However, she feels bad that she often does not have the time she would like to devote to prayer, as her family and job responsibilities sometimes crowd her more than she wants. She feels happy that she is married, but wishes that her spouse and children would be more considerate of her desire for some time alone with the Lord. They are quite demanding of her time and attention and feel that her job is to take care of them and to cater to their needs and wishes.

Jennifer always was taught that a woman's job was just that, to be totally available to her husband and children at all times, but now she is beginning to question this principle and wonders whether that can square with God's claim on her life. How should Jennifer be advised about juggling prayer time and family and work time?

Underlying meaning: Often a devout woman will encounter this problem. It seems that there is no easy solution, yet common sense can assist the directee in knowing when to devote time to explicit prayer and when to tend to other responsibilities. There should be a sense of priorities. Of course, God comes first but sometimes, if we have certain responsibilities, he is asking us to see and serve him in others, instead of running to church all the time.

Suggestions: Many people who are pressed for time and yet want to spend some time with the Lord, every day if possible, will have to exercise some self-discipline and perhaps cut into their TV or sleep time. Many of us would be amazed how much time we spend watching TV, reading the paper, looking for bargains, or talking on the phone. It easily could be devoted to prayer instead.

It is a matter of perhaps not watching the late show on TV and going to sleep a little earlier, to wake up early and keep our daily rendezvous with the Lord. Those who truly love the Lord won't usually be called to sacrifice their families and jobs, but rather some of the frivolous things that unnecessarily take up so much time. What about praying in a traffic jam instead of fussing and fuming? Then there is the waiting for doctors, dentists, etc., when we can do some spiritual reading. I believe that for those who want to be with the Lord, there is usually a way to make that possible.

Tongues

Difficulties presented: Michelle has been going to a charismatic prayer meeting and some of the members there are encouraging her to try to speak in tongues. Michelle wonders what the value is of this practice or whether it is an authentic gift of the Spirit, and also whether its possession is necessary in order to be a Christian. She has tried to speak in tongues and has thus far been unsuccessful. She feels fearful that maybe this is a sign that she is not a real Christian. How would you respond?

Underlying meaning: A person who wants the gift of tongues might very well receive it, as St. Paul lists it among the gifts of the Holy Spirit. Many people have found that the practice of praying in tongues has helped them in their prayer life, especially when they run out of words in which to pray. However, it is not the greatest of the gifts, and it is not necessary to possess this gift in order to be a Christian (1 Cor 12-14).

Suggestions: Encourage Michelle to be open to the working of the Holy Spirit. Explain that the gift of tongues is a legitimate gift, but that the Christian life does not stand or fall with it. Sometimes, Michelle can be told, a person gets a couple of sounds or words and then with the exercise of the gift, the sounds or words are increased. We have to cooperate with the Lord to some extent in some cases in order to receive the gift.

Unanswered Prayer

Difficulties presented: Amber had put all of her hope in God and asked that God be her Everything. Now it seems that he has let Amber down and left fervent prayers and her heart's desires go unanswered. She wonders why God could be so cruel. Doesn't God know that she was trying to put God first, put all of her eggs in one basket, and God has now let her down?

Underlying meaning: We sometimes tend to think that if we do all of the right things and say all of the right prayers, that God has to provide the answers that we desire. How disappointed we are when things don't work out the way we had hoped! Yet sometimes, even if the request is legitimate, God might just have a better way. Sometimes we ourselves tend to get in the way of what God wants to do by not preparing ourselves adequately to receive his answer. It's like the man who prayed to win the lotto but didn't buy a ticket.

Suggestions: Explain to Amber that God's ways aren't our ways (Is 55:8-9), that sometimes he permits failure, disappointment, sickness, etc., to lead us from the cross to a new resurrection. Maybe he is doing this to be recognized as the source of our good fortune, so we won't attribute it to good luck, the stars, etc. We can depend on his Word that he is faithful and promised never to desert us or fail us (see Heb 13). Encourage Amber to give herself to the Lord and allow the Lord to assuage the pain of disappointment through his healing love, communicated through prayer.

Visions

Difficulties presented: Janice claims to have had a vision of the Sacred Heart and of the Blessed Mother. The vision was very beautiful, but she wonders whether she should accept it and/or believe in it. She has heard that you have to be careful in accepting visions, as it is easy to be deceived. However, she fears that if she doesn't believe in its reality, Jesus and the Blessed Mother will be offended. She doesn't want to hurt Jesus and Mary and so is not sure how to act or what to believe. Janice also wonders if she is a special person to the Lord because of having been the recipient of the vision. How would you counsel Janice in this situation and try to answer her questions?

Underlying meaning: It is true that visions from the Lord are possible, but we shouldn't be too eager to believe that every mental perception is a true divine vision, and we shouldn't think we are better than others. St. Teresa of Avila reminds us that Jesus even spoke (and we might add, appeared) to the Pharisees (cf. *Life* 25; *Interior Castle* VI:3:1ff). But that doesn't mean that they were necessarily his friends or that they were the holiest people. Even if we really had a vision, it doesn't mean that we're almost in heaven. It could be that we are especially needy and that therefore the Lord is allowing himself to be known by us in this lowly fashion—for visions are not the most spiritual type of communication that exists. More advanced is walking by faith, devoid of all consolations, yet believing in God's love, even if we feel, see or hear nothing at all—that is, if we are to believe St. John of the Cross.

Fr. Benedict Groeschel in his book, *A Still, Small Voice,* also writes extensively about what spiritual directors should do when directees claim to have unusual experiences of the Lord. The book is highly recommended to anyone who wants to study this topic of visions, locutions, and other purported divine revelations.

Suggestions: It would be good to be prudent and follow the guidelines spelled out by Sts. Teresa of Avila and John of the Cross on the discernment of locutions (*Life* 25; *Interior Castle* VI:3:1ff; *Ascent* II: 28-30), which can also be applied to a great extent to the discernment of visions (see heading: Locutions).

Vocation

Difficulties presented: Blanche, a mother of five children, comes to see you because she feels that God is calling her to the foreign missions. She and her husband are barely making it financially, but she is confident that they can raise enough money to go and be missionaries in Africa or South America. She feels that she is not doing enough at the present time, and that the people in the foreign missions are more needy than she and her husband and children could ever be in the United States.

She has always wanted to do something great for the Lord and now God has called her to do what is needed in the world. She says that the Blessed Mother spoke to her about it, and that she is sure that it will work out if they have enough faith and obey the Lord. She is convinced that God has always provided for their needs, if not for all of their wants. How would you counsel her?

Underlying meaning: Normally speaking, it is good to follow our common sense in listening to spiritual vibes. Common sense is especially needed if we have a lot of responsibility, like that of caring for a family, which is our first responsibility, even though it might not be as exciting as doing interesting things in other countries.

Suggestions: If this sense of calling persists, it might be good to talk it over with a spiritual director, but in the meantime, it is advisable to write down the pros and cons of such a venture. We can also pray for the Lord to send someone else, or try to sponsor someone who is going to the foreign missions. Maybe, if we really feel called, after thinking and praying about it for a period of several weeks or months, we can try it during our vacation, as this often can be arranged—that is, to go abroad and see what it's like at a mission site. If we still feel called, then perhaps it is meant for further down the road, when we have fewer family and financial responsibilities.

Vocation

Difficulties presented: A married woman named Alma comes to you for spiritual direction because she feels God is calling her to the celibate life, perhaps in the convent. She has discussed this with her husband, but he is reluctant to let her go. She feels that she can do more good in the world and church if only she could be celibate. Also, she feels that she will be more able to devote herself to a life of intense prayer without the distractions of married and domestic life. She is sad that he does not perceive the will of the Lord like she does, and asks you to intervene and help her to convince him to let her be a nun. What should you do?

Underlying meaning: On occasion it could happen that God is calling a married person to the religious life. However, this is rare, and because of the prior commitment of marriage, the woman who wants to be a nun cannot do so without her husband's consent. This would pose an almost intolerable burden on the husband, and unless they both want to pursue religious life, it may not be feasible. It is questionable if it is really the Lord who is calling the woman to religious life, although perhaps someday circumstances will allow it, i.e., if she becomes a widow and her children, if any, are grown, then she would be free to pursue this type of a vocation. Maybe it is an indication of what is further down the road, but not for now.

Suggestions: Make this woman aware of the fact that God loves her in a very special way that she would want to be a nun, but that within marriage there are also many opportunities to be close to God in a felt way, and to serve and glorify him. Gently explain to her that unless her husband willingly concedes for her to become a nun, and perhaps wants to enter religious life himself, she is bound to her first commitment of marriage and can't go off and do something else with her life. It might be a hard struggle, but with the help of God's grace, and with prayer (maybe together), the marriage can be an aid to a deeper union with God, perhaps with her husband becoming closer to the Lord also.

List of Recommended Readings

Arterburn, Stephen and Jack Felton. *Faith that Hurts, Faith that Heals*. Nashville, TN: Thomas Nelson Publishers, 1991.

Aumann, Jordan. *Spiritual Theology*. Westminster, MD: Christian Classics, Inc., 1980.

Aune, David E. *Prophecy in Early Christianity and the Ancient Mediterranean World*. Grand Rapids, MI: Eerdmans, 1983.

Barry, William A. and William J. Connolly. *The Practice of Spiritual Direction*. San Francisco: Harper & Row, 1982.

Benner, David G., ed. *Psychology and Religion*. Grand Rapids, MI: Baker House, 1988.

Bielecki, Tessa. *Holy Daring, An Outrageous Gift to Modern Spirituality from St. Teresa, the Grand Wild Woman of Avila*. Rockport, MA: Element, 1994.

Boucher, John J. *Is Talking to God a Long Distance Call? How to Hear and Understand God's Voice*. Ann Arbor, MI: Servant Publications, 1990.

Browning, Don S. *Religious Thought and the Modern Psycholo-*

gies, A Critical Conversation in the Theology of Culture. Philadelphia: Fortress Press, 1987.

Clinebell, Howard J., Jr. *Basic Types of Pastoral Counseling.* Nashville, TN: Abingdon Press, 1966.

Conroy, Maureen. *Looking into the Well: Supervision of Spiritual Directors.* Chicago: Loyola University Press, 1995.

Conroy, Maureen. *The Discerning Heart, Discovering a Personal God.* Chicago: Loyola University Press, 1993.

Cronk, Sandra. *Dark Night Journey: Inward Repatterning Toward a Life Centered in God.* Wallingford, PA: Pendle Hill Publications, 1991.

Cummins, Norbert. *Freedom to Rejoice: Understanding St. John of the Cross.* San Francisco: HarperCollins, 1991.

Dubay, Thomas. *The Fire Within: St. Teresa of Avila, St. John of the Cross and the Gospel on Prayer.* San Francisco: Ignatius Press, 1989.

Dunne, Tad. *Spiritual Mentoring, Guiding People through Spiritual Exercises to Life Decisions.* San Francisco: HarperCollins, 1991.

Granfield, David. *Heightened Consciousness, the Mystical Difference.* Mahwah, NJ: Paulist Press, 1991.

Gratton, Carolyn. *The Art of Spiritual Guidance.* New York: Crossroad, 1993.

Groeschel, Benedict. *A Still Small Voice.* San Francisco: Ignatius Press, 1993.

Groeschel, Benedict. *Stumbling Blocks or Stepping Stones, Spiritual Answers to Psychological Questions.* Mahwah, NJ: Paulist Press, 1989.

Johnston, William. *Lord, Teach Us to Pray: Christian Zen and the Inner Eye of Love.* San Francisco: HarperCollins, 1990.

Johnston, William. *Mystical Theology, The Science of Love.* San Francisco, CA: HarperCollins, 1995.

Johnston, William. *The Still Point, Reflections on Zen and Christian Mysticism.* New York, NY: Fordham University Press, 1982.

Kavanaugh, Kieran and Otilio Rodriguez, eds. *The Collected Works of St. John of the Cross.* Washington, DC: ICS Publications, 1979.

Kavanaugh, Kieran and Otilio Rodriguez, eds. *The Collected Works of St. Teresa of Avila,* Vols. 1 & 2, Washington, DC: ICS Publications, 1980.

Kelsey, Morton T. *Companions on the Inner Way: The Art of Spiritual Guidance.* New York: Crossroad, 1991.

Liebert, Elizabeth. *Changing Life Patterns. Adult Development in Spiritual Direction.* Mahwah, NJ: Paulist Press, 1992.

Lloyd-Jones, D. Martyn. *Spiritual Depression, Its Causes and Its Cure.* Grand Rapids, MI: Eerdmans, 1965, 1988.

Lozano, John M. *Praying Even When the Door Seems Closed: The Nature and Stages of Prayer.* Mahwah, NJ: Paulist Press, 1989.

Malony, H. Newton. *Psychology of Religion, Personalities, Problems, Possibilities.* Grand Rapids, MI: Baker Book House, 1991.

Maritain, Jacques. *The Degrees of Knowledge.* Notre Dame, IN: University of Notre Dame Press, 1995.

May, Gerald G., M.D. *Will and Spirit, A Contemplative Psychology.* San Francisco: Harper & Row, 1982.

Muto, Susan. *John of the Cross for Today: The Dark Night.* Notre Dame, IN: Ave Maria Press, 1994.

Nemeck, Francis Kelly and Marie Theresa Coombs. *Contemplation.* Wilmington, DE: Michael Glazier, Inc., 1982.

————. *The Spiritual Journey, Critical Thresholds and Stages of Adult Spiritual Genesis.* Wilmington, DE: Michael Glazier, Inc., 1987.

————. *The Way of Spiritual Direction.* Wilmington, DE: Michael Glazier, Inc., 1985.

Neufelder, Jerome M. and Mary C. Coelho, eds. *Writings on Spiritual Direction by Great Christian Masters.* Minneapolis, MN: The Seabury Press, 1982.

Oden, Thomas C. *The Transforming Power of Grace.* Nashville, TN: Abingdon Press, 1993.

Rohrbach, Peter Thomas. *Coversation with Christ: The Teaching of St. Teresa of Avila About Personal Prayer.* Rockford, IL: Tan Books and Publishers, Inc., 1980.

Ruffing, Janet. *Uncovering Stories of Faith: Spiritual Direction and Narrative.* Mahwah, NJ: Paulist Press, 1989.

Stephens, Dr. Larry D. *Please Let Me Know You, God.* Nashville, TN: Thomas Nelson Publishers, 1993.

90 HANDBOOK FOR SPIRITUAL DIRECTORS

Sullender, R. Scott. *Grief and Growth: Pastoral Resources for Emotional and Spiritual Growth.* Mahwah, NJ: Paulist Press, 1985.

Taylor, Charles W. *The Skilled Pastor, Counseling as the Practice of Theology.* Minneapolis, MN: Fortress Press, 1991.

Toner, Jules. *A Commentary on St. Ignatius' Rules for the Discernment of Spirits.* St. Louis, MO: The Institute of Jesuit Sources, 1982.

Van Kaam, Adrian. *Foundations for Personality Study, An Adrian van Kaam Reader.* Denville, NJ: Dimension Books, Inc., 1983.

Walters, Jack. *Jesus, Healer of Our Inner World.* New York: Crossroad, 1995.

Welch, John. *Spiritual Pilgrims, Carl Jung and Teresa of Avila.* Mahwah, NJ: Paulist Press, 1982.

Welch, John. *When Gods Die.* Mahwah, NJ: Paulist Press, 1990.

Wicks, Robert J., ed. *Handbook of Spirituality for Ministers.* Mahwah, NJ: Paulist Press, 1995.

Willard, Dallas. *In Search of Guidance, Developing a Conversational Relationship with God.* San Francisco: HarperCollins, 1993.

Wright, H. Norman. *Self-Talk, Imagery, and Prayer in Counseling.* Waco, TX: Word Books, 1986.

Yancey, Philip. *Disappointment with God.* Grand Rapids, MI: Zondervan, 1988.

Yandel, Keith E. *The Epistemology of Religious Experience.* New York: Cambridge University Press, 1993.